WISDOM
OF THE
LITTLE FLOWER

Thérèse of Lisieux–
Bearer of Western
Spirituality

RUDOLF STERTENBRINK

Translated by Peter Heinegg

A Crossroad Book
The Crossroad Publishing Company
New York

The Crossroad Publishing Company
481 Eighth Avenue, New York, NY 10001

First published as *Die große Liebe des kleinen Senfkorns: Begegnung mit Thérèse von Lisieux, der neuen Kirchenlehrein*, copyright © 2002 by Verlag Herder, Freiburg im Breisgau

English translation copyright © 2002 by The Crossroad Publishing Company

Printed in the United States of America

Cataloging-in-Publication Data is available from the Library of Congress

ISBN 0-8245-1983-3

1 2 3 4 5 6 7 8 9 10   10 09 08 07 06 05 04 03 02

Contents

There are so many aspects

to the message of Thérèse of Lisieux.

Perhaps each one who gets to know her writings

learns something a little different,

something very personally suited

to one's own needs.

— Benedict J. Groeschel

I

HOW TO GET IN TOUCH
WITH GOD

1 Those Who Listen, Live

One day Rabbi Yehoshua ben Levi asked the prophet Elijah, "When will the Messiah come?"

Elijah answered: "Go and ask him yourself."

He went to him and greeted him: "Peace be with you, Master and teacher!"

"Peace be with you, son of Levi!" the Messiah answered.

"When will you come, Master?"

"Today."

Later Rabbi Yehoshua ben Levi complained to Elijah: "The Messiah lied to me. He said he would come today and he didn't."

But Elijah said: "You misunderstood him. He simply quoted Psalm 95, verse 7: 'Oh, that today you would hearken to his voice.' "[1]

Let's add to this verse the following: "Harden not your hearts, as at Meribah, as on the day of Massah in the wilderness."

Whenever our hearts become hardened, our lives wilt. "Life" in the real sense means blooming, unfolding, opening up, overcoming, growing, transforming. We are alive only as long as we are open and receptive to God's word. Whence the earnest note in the line from the Psalm: "Oh, that today you would hearken to his voice." When that happens, God is on the way.

~

Meister Eckhart says, "God works on us to the degree that he finds us ready. . . . There is a parallel in nature: when one heats an oven and places three batches of dough in it — one made with oats, another made with barley, and another made with rye — there is only one source of heat in the oven, and yet it does not have the same effect on the different doughs: The one becomes a fine loaf, the other a coarser kind, and the third still coarser. But it's not the heat's fault; it's the fault of the material, which is uneven. As with the bread, God does not work the same way in all hearts; he works on us to the degree that he finds readiness and receptiveness."[2]

Jesus addresses this topic still more simply, precisely, and profoundly. He begins more or less this way: "The human heart is like a very varied field, in which the seed [that is, the word of God] is to come." He then names the three groups that refuse the word of God (Matt. 13:1–9).

The first group is composed of those whose hearts are like a well-beaten path. The seeds that fall on such a path are soon snatched away by the birds. With people of this sort the inner organ for everything religious is stunted. The world beyond strikes them as something unreal.

The second group are the superficial ones, whose hearts are like rocky ground with little soil. The seed springs up immediately, but the sprout quickly wilts beneath the sun because it can't form any deep roots. Such people are open to everything, but they don't let themselves be really moved. Nothing sends down roots. They lack depth; they flee from resistance and criticism. Ignatius Loyola tells us: "It is a fact of experience that the greatest fruits are to be hoped for exactly where the most vigorous resistance arises." The superficial ones don't agree with this conviction; they always seek the easier path. Unsteadiness and a lack of persistence are hallmarks of this type of person.

In the third group we find the defeated. They are like the thorns that fall in among the seeds. The thorns grow and stifle the wheat. Such people have struggled sincerely; they have principles and try to live by them. They are presenting a façade and they don't just pretend. They are absolutely authentic. But then something else presses into the foreground, and religion fades away.

Jesus contrasts these three unreceptive groups with three groups of open-minded persons: "Other seeds fell on good soil and brought forth grain, some a hundred-fold, some sixty, some thirty" (Matt. 13:8).

In the first place are the hundred-percenters. These are the whole and undivided ones, the saints. They have put God in the first place of their life, and everything else comes after that. Externally they have many failures, but under their touch everything grows toward eternal life.

The second group, the sixty-percenters, also win praise from the Lord. They have fought and are wounded in life's toils. But as fighters they belong with the victorious. They are struggling and maturing. In their distress and in their defeat they keep looking to God and turning to him. A man once told me, "If at the end of my life I can't stand before God as a winner, then at least let it be as a fighter."

Even the third group, the thirty-percenters, gets recognition from the Lord. Their faith is a daily up-and-down. Their religious life has its ebbs and flows, its progress and backsliding. Bright days stand alongside dark nights. It is by no means taken for granted that everything will come out well in the end, but they stick with Jesus. In trust in his forgiving love they continually confess their guilt. They do it with the confidence that God can still create something worthwhile, even out of their guilt.

~

Thus, in Jesus' address the group of the hardened souls and the group of the receptive souls face each other. Both are like a field on which God's seed is cast. But both are not open to receiving him in themselves. Which group do I belong to? The answer is provided on the path to silence, because it is above all in silence that the soul opens up to the truth. In silence it purifies itself from everything that makes it selfish, hard, and unreceptive. Anyone who talks a lot puts himself in the center of things in order to show himself to good advantage. But in this very way he falls away from his center. Thérèse writes in one of her numerous letters:

Silence does the soul good.

Then there is the fact that thoughtless talk takes away the soul's inner wakefulness. Thérèse says:

A soul without silence is like a city without guards.

An old monastic father makes the point with the following image: "As the constantly open gates of the bathhouse very quickly let the warmth inside flow outside, those who talk a great deal let their inner strength escape through the door of their voice." The energy that lets us turn a good intention into action is lost. This is confirmed by the saying of Søren Kierkegaard: "Whatever I talk about I don't do." We can understand why Thérèse says:

Whoever cultivates silence preserves his soul.

Without silence the soul gets sick. It becomes recalcitrant and unfruitful, which is why many people today have rediscovered silence as a cure for their seeking souls.

In Thérèse's case, silence was a basic attitude of her life. Even her sister Pauline (Sr. Agnès de Jésus) didn't find out about the severe illness that led to Thérèse's early death until months afterward. Thérèse kept silent so that she could hear the God who instructs without the noise of words. Besides, she was aware that there are things "that lose their fragrance as soon as they are exposed to the air." She clearly perceived that the soul is made more for silence than for speech. It is silence that opens our ears and enables us to hear.

In the prophet Isaiah we read: "Hear, that your soul may live." By hearing, we come to life. So, too, those who don't hear don't know what life is all about. The listening person makes out what is important to the other person, and to God.

2   Discovering the Child Within

A person's openness and receptiveness to God and his word grow out of the silence that makes listening possible.

In his *Edifying Discourses*, Søren Kierkegaard questions from whom we can learn this silence and listening.[3] His answer is that one of the first models God gave us of "listening silence" and "silent listening" is woman. Kierkegaard sees the essence of piety in femininity. Silence before God can be learned from women.

Silent listening is also part of a faith that doesn't ask, in doubt or mistrust, "Why?" "What for?" "How is that possible?" Rather it speaks as Mary did: "Behold, I am the handmaid of the Lord" (Luke 1:38). Anyone who speaks that way keeps silent. Although Mary didn't understand the words, she kept them in her heart — that is, she didn't insist on understanding God's word. Rather, she kept the word silently in her good heart, waiting till the meaning dawned on her.

In Mary we plainly see how a person can come to rest in God's presence despite a deep and heavy suffering, and be capable of silence even when in severe pain.

Much as woman stands in the Bible for silent listening, for receptiveness, for piety and trust in God, the Bible has yet another image for the openness without which God cannot give us his gifts. It is the child whom the Bible calls blessed, and being a child is at the center of Thérèse's spirituality. It's appropriate to probe a little more deeply into the essence of the child.

At the beginning of the *Treatise on the Passions of Love*, which has been attributed to Blaise Pascal (1623–62) there is the following statement: "The life of man is terribly short. It is usually reckoned from the day of birth onward. As for myself, I would have it begin only with the awakening of reason, when one begins to let oneself be guided by reason, which seldom happens before the twentieth year of life. Before that one is only a child."

The author of this remark exaggerates the value of the calculating understanding of adults and underestimates the value of the child's trusting heart. Pascal increasingly lost trust in his own knowledge and, as Abbé Beurrier, the priest who heard his last confession, said, "He had become simple like a little child."

Whoever the author of the *Treatise* was, one could hardly imagine a statement more contrary to the conviction of Thérèse of Lisieux. She wanted nothing else than to become more and more a child in the presence of God.

A child knows that it is nothing in and of itself, that it has nothing and can do nothing. This awareness leads to the perspective that is the most childlike thing about the child. The child looks up because it expects everything to come from there. Thus, the child's heart becomes wide and bright as it looks up. Thérèse was fully conscious of this.

The more grown-up a person becomes, the greater the danger that his or her perspective will be shifted from above to below and thereby become increasingly narrow, dark, and hard. Think of the passage in the Gospel of Luke: "Now they were bringing even infants to him that he might touch them; and when the disciples saw it, they rebuked them. But Jesus called them to him, saying, 'Let the children come to me, and do not hinder them; for to such belongs the kingdom of God. Truly, I say to you: whoever does not receive the kingdom of God like a child shall not enter it" (Luke 18:15–17).

Why did the disciples turn the people down so harshly? Perhaps they had lost contact with the child within themselves. We always deal with others the way we deal with the child in us. A person is healthy if the child in him lives and is given breathing space, for the most childlike thing in the child is at the same time the most human part of the human being.

Who is it within us who believes, hopes, loves, prays, and trusts? Who is it within us who weeps and laughs? It is the child who lives at the bottom of our heart. Discover the child in you; this child is the most divine part of you, the part that most resembles the Creator. Whoever wants to grow and truly ripen toward his or her true essence has to make contact with the child within and lead it to the good, to God.

This is the characteristic quality of "the little way of spiritual childhood." Whoever discovers the child in herself and has made the child's upward gaze her essential look is saved from dependence upon the past and fear of the future. It becomes possible for her to live in "God's today." Cultivate the child in yourself by looking up to the Infinite, living in God's today, and giving yourself fully to what you are assigned to do here and now.

～

In her spiritual childhood, Thérèse of Lisieux, in the few years of her earthly life, achieved a state of mastery. Those who imitate her spirituality feel in themselves "the longing arise for greatness and holiness, the longing that follows the acquaintance with exquisite individuals."[4]

At the center of Thérèsian spirituality stands the concept of being a child in the presence of God. It is the highest and most mysterious of all relationships. Thérèse boldly shed light on what it means for God to love the child in every person unconditionally.

Anyone who penetrates to this trust will find the Gospel to be a message of joy and discover what is great in what is little. Thérèse was able to do this because she did not think but, first and foremost, saw. She intuitively grasped the connections and formulated them in spare, measured phrases or apt images. The Swiss theologian Hans Urs von Balthasar said, "I know of no Christian canonized in recent years who had such a poetic ability as Thérèse of Lisieux. The images somehow pour forth from her pen, always original, always on target. That is how she illustrates her teaching...which is colorful, understandable, and appealing."[5] The following image offers evidence of this:

For some time I had offered myself to Jesus, to be his little toy. I told him he should make use of me, not like a valuable toy that children only look at, but like a little ball that he could throw on the floor, kick, drill a hole through, leave in a corner, or press to his heart.

Such simplicity is possible only on the basis of an unconditional trust in God.

3 Our Future Grows Out of Our Connections

What gives our life a certain explosiveness are those unforeseen situations that open our eyes to a hitherto hidden truth. We find ourselves pensively asking: Who would have thought?

This often happens to us with people whom we think we know. There are men and women we like because of their outward appearance; we feel connected to them. But sometimes we are forced to realize that behind an attractive exterior lies nothing that corresponds to it. In disappointment we wonder: Who would have thought?

But fortunately the opposite occurs as well: we meet people we take to be insignificant, but who then reveal a hidden richness that stuns us. All at once it comes to us: much that *doesn't* glitter is gold nonetheless. Here, too, we pensively ask: Who would have thought?

One such person who but gains the more intensively one deals with her is Thérèse. Her life shows how everything can change unbelievably if one opens oneself to

God, thinks of oneself as a child before him, and lets oneself be penetrated and held by his love.

~

Lisieux, once a rather old-fashioned little town in Normandy with half-timbered, pointed, gabled houses and slightly more than fifteen thousand inhabitants, wasn't especially well known until it burst into the spotlight and became the second greatest pilgrimage site, after Lourdes, in all of France.

Thérèse was born on January 2, 1873, in Alençon, sixty miles south of Lisieux, the ninth child in a family with the very common name of Martin. The father was a watchmaker and had a jewelry shop; the mother ran a lace store. When Thérèse was five years old, her mother died of breast cancer. Shortly afterward her father moved to Lisieux with his five daughters (the other children had died at an early age). It was an insignificant person who was destined to bring worldwide status to this little town. Who would have thought?

Thérèse never finished school. She was taught by her elder sister Pauline, who had become her second mother, until at age nine she went to the school run by the Benedictine nuns in Lisieux as a half-day pupil.

She left it after five years and was then tutored by an elderly lady.

Another of Thérèse's sisters, Céline, who after her father's death had likewise entered the Carmelites, said: "She was so reserved that even her relatives thought she was insignificant and said, 'Since she entered the convent too young, her faulty education will be noticed for the rest of her life.'" And yet, with neither a satisfactory formal education nor theological training, she gave new impulses to theology. Some of the most noted theologians took up her ideas, and still do. And — something no one would have ever thought possible — on October 19, 1997, Pope John Paul II elevated her to Doctor of the Church.

At fifteen, she wanted to enter the Carmelite convent in Lisieux, which her two elder sisters Marie and Pauline had already entered, but she was refused because of her youth. On October 31, 1887, she called on the bishop of Bayeux for help, but without success. A few days later she went with her father and her sister Céline on a pilgrimage to Rome that lasted until December 2, 1887. At an audience with Pope Leo XIII for a group of pilgrims on November 20, 1887, Thérèse personally addressed the pope: "Most Holy Father, in honor of your jubilee allow me to enter Carmel at fifteen."

Vicar General Révérony, who had been an assistant to Bishop Hugonin since 1878 and who knew of the girl's plan, had forbidden the pilgrims to speak to the pope. Now he interrupted her and explained to Leo XIII: "Most Holy Father, this is a child who would like to enter the Carmelites at the age of fifteen. The superiors are currently looking into the matter." The pope told Thérèse: "You will enter when the good Lord wills." Then two Swiss Guards dragged her away from the feet of the pope, with the help of Abbé Révérony.

Thérèse would be beatified thirty-six years later, in 1923, and canonized in 1925. In 1980, Pope John Paul II made a pilgrimage to Lisieux to honor this youthful saint.

When Thérèse entered the Carmelites on April 8, 1888, Monsignor Delatroëtte, the convent's spiritual director, told the prioress: "On behalf of the most reverend bishop I am handing over to you this fifteen-year-old child, whose entrance you have requested. I hope she doesn't disappoint your hopes; but I call your attention to the fact that you alone bear the responsibility if things work out differently from what you expect." Things did work out quite differently. Who would have thought?

There is a well-known anecdote reported by Thérèse's biographer Ida Friederike Görres: "During the final months of her illness, while lying in her sickroom, Thérèse heard one nun saying to another: 'Sister Thérèse is going to die soon. What will our Mother Prioress ever be able to write in her obituary notice? She joined us, lived, and died — there really isn't anything more to say." Then *The Story of a Soul*, Thérèse's autobiography, became a sensation and was translated into practically all the major languages of the world.

"My burial place means little to me," Thérèse said. "Let it be wherever, what difference does it make? So many missionaries have been buried in the stomachs of cannibals." Today the remains of the saint rest in the monumental basilica that was erected in her honor and consecrated in 1938 by Eugenio Pacelli, the future Pope Pius XII. The precious reliquary was donated by Pope Pius XI.

~

How can we explain this transformation from someone inconspicuous and unprepossessing to someone who could not be ignored, this transformation from nothing to everything? Perhaps we can see what "Providence" means.

Providence is part of the core of Jesus' preaching. It means that whatever happens in the world is directed by the love, wisdom, and kindness of God for the salvation of the believer. Jesus spoke with special urgency about it in the Sermon on the Mount (Matt. 6:24–34). There he encourages his listeners not to worry about food and clothing, since their Father in heaven knows what people need. Believers were to trust in the way the Father took care of them.

Jesus didn't mean that a believer could just ignore all needs and float along because wondrous powers were taking care of everything. Jesus had in view the entire reality of existence and overlooked none of its painful features. What Jesus meant above all is that the living God loves every individual and cares for him or her personally. Augustine puts it this way: "The one who made you also knows what he wants to do with you."

The Sermon on the Mount points to the birds in the skies. Whatever food they need comes to them. Then our eyes are directed to the flowers of the field, which don't need to worry about their beauty. All this must have sounded like a pious fairy tale, but it is followed by a directive that shows how deeply serious Jesus was: "Seek first his kingdom and his righteousness, and all these things shall be yours as well" (Matt. 6:33).

This saying links God's loving Providence with the faithful attachment of human beings. When a person's search is aimed first of all at the kingdom of God, everything else comes along. What happens in a person's life depends on how much room he or she makes in it for God's workings. "A deeper knowledge of human beings also shows how precisely the inner mindset of the personality, often quite unconsciously, shapes the course of their destiny" (Romano Guardini).

Jesus' message about Providence challenges us to make concern for God's kingdom the first concern of our lives. At the same time, and always in advance of them, our efforts will be matched by God's concern for us and our salvation. There is also a general providence, thanks to which God holds in his hands everything that happens in the world, even when human beings pay no attention whatever to the kingdom of God. Jesus is our guarantee that God does not simply leave the world and the human race to their own devices, while he looks idly on.

The message about Providence in the Sermon on the Mount is important to us precisely because Thérèse abandoned herself completely to the will of God and his guidance.

The honor of Jesus is my only ambition, I leave my own honor to him. And if he seems to have forgotten me, well, he is free to do so; because I no longer belong to myself, but to him. . . .

What a connection, what a future!

These statements give us some idea of the mystery of her life from the perspective of divine Providence.

4 "I Have Only One Wish, and That Is You"

There are many ways to learn about the uniqueness, capabilities, and characteristic features of another person. We can mediate, for example, on that person's dreams or study that person's handwriting. Let's look at what Thérèse says about her dreams:

If my dreams come true someday, I'll live in the country. When I think about my plans, I feel transported to an enchanting little house or a sunny chalet. All my rooms look out on the sea, because my little house would be in a village on the seashore. My garden would be rather large. Behind the garden would be a meadow with a barn. My greenhouse would always be full of the loveliest flowers. I would have a little boat, so I could occasionally take a trip on the sea.

Thérèse had an extraordinary talent for observation, an unusually fine ear, and highly developed aesthetic sensitivity. In her believing childlikeness she experienced the world as creation, in which everything resounded. It was not just the sun that resounded, as Goethe said, but every creature — flowers, animals, and children. Thérèse understood their language and heard their melody. This reminds me of a quatrain by Joseph von Eichendorff, entitled "The Divining Rod":

> A song's asleep in every thing,
> As they slumber forth and forth.
> The world itself begins to sing,
> Once you find the magic word.

There is a song lying dormant in everything, which we could hear if we knew how to awaken it. Whoever manages to do so will experience the world in a wholly new way. If that is true, the magic word would be the most important word in our lives.

Some time ago I was talking with friends on a summer evening. Someone asked, "What is the most important word in your life?" The answers were as varied as the faces around the table. By the end there was only one student who hadn't responded. "You haven't said anything yet," he was told. He caught his breath for a moment and said, "The most important word there is for any person is YOU."

YOU is the magic word that awakens the song in everything. Whoever has found, like a child, a personal relationship to everything will learn how all things come to her and open up to her, allowing her to share in their inner mystery. In his memoir *Look Up to the Stars — Pay Attention to the Streets*, Jörg Zink recalls the time when he was seven years old: "Back then I talked with everything I met, with bugs and with moss, with stones and with springs. Everything was alive, and I myself was no different from them."[6]

But Thérèse's sensibility ran still deeper, because in each and every thing she sensed the presence of the divine YOU, through whose word everything was created. For Thérèse, everything contains a message — so we can learn something from everything. For the same reason, all things point beyond themselves. They are signposts to the Eternal, which greets us from far away.

When Thérèse felt touched by the Eternal — at the sight of the ocean or the setting sun or fields of wheat, she felt homesickness. At such moments she wanted to be by herself, for these were moments when she was filled with profound thoughts, and she lost herself in meditation.

I have always loved what is great and beautiful.

———

What to say about Thérèse's handwriting? The many graphologists who have looked at it agree. Their conclusions frequently repeat one another and run as follows: "The intelligence is that of a towering personality. A decidedly masculine intellect is connected to a highly sensitive, profound feminine emotional structure with an unusual charm. With her artistic sense of life she lovingly discovers greatness precisely in what is little. The world of her perceptions is rich and so particular that one can infer a feminine originality of an extraordinary scope. She has an admirable gift for grasping immediately the beauties of nature. Her lyrical gift lets her intuitively find images of lofty linguistic expressive power.

"But there is also an unmistakable self-centeredness, which is not without its dangers, and a strong ambition. She knows that she is beautiful, and she knows how to make herself beautiful. She does this not only to please herself, but others as well. She feels joy when people admire her. She can't bear standing somewhere in the background. She would like to be recognized. People should busy themselves with her somehow or other. If she were not to resist these weaknesses, she would place herself at the center of things even in the convent.

"She is well-mannered and knows how to present herself. Since she always strives for the greatest possible fulfillment, she will experience many disappointments. Her willpower quickly crumbles when her wishes and hopes can't be realized. Fear and depression result from her disappointment, which can reach the stage of making her physically sick. Because of her impressionability every joyful or painful experience throw her out of balance."[7]

Most of the observations expressed in these graphological studies can also be found in the writings of the saint. Thérèse was surely aware of her flaws. Later we will see how she worked on herself so as to become the mistress and not the slave of her weaknesses. In the report of a Roman graphologist, who often consulted at canonization trials, there is a note that points out the direction in which she sought to improve herself. "In the subject's handwriting, finally, there is revealed yet another peculiar feature. Most of the words end with an extremely thin, as it were spiritual, stroke, which takes three different forms. Sometimes this stroke will lie flat as if on the floor, sometimes it will shoot up and curl back again in a fine curve, and sometimes again it will stretch out like an offertory plate.

"What are we to make of this unusual phenomenon? The writer keeps identifying in her thoughts with the Absolute. At first humble and pleading, the second time joyfully rising up to it, and then again returning to work, the third time offering herself to the Absolute, in order to receive its love. Thus we recognize from these characters that the writer feels constantly connected to the Absolute. She strives in this way to subordinate her self-centeredness, her drivenness, and her sensuality to the Absolute, now pleading, now loving, now giving herself entirely away."[8]

~

The life of St. Thérèse shows that we are not irresistibly compelled by our nature, our dispositions, or our drives to develop in a certain direction. We are often tempted to blame our peculiar characteristics for our being this way or that. To be sure, our character has a profound influence on the course of our development. But this does not mean that we can develop only in a certain way and not in another. Rather, our character provides the material from which we can give shape to many things.

How did Thérèse manage to avoid becoming the prisoner of her nature, her drives, and her passions? She tried to grow beyond herself. In the process she sensed that unless God helped her this would never happen, or only with difficulty. Out of this experience grew a longing:

I have only one wish, and that is you, my God.

This is a good prayer. It shows how intent Thérèse was on letting God have the first place in her life, and it corresponds to the first of the Ten Commandments. Whoever fulfills it is not far from holiness. But what does it mean to put God in the first place of one's life? Thérèse answers:

I wish to be the prisoner of your love.

The prisoner has no will of her own. Those who abandon their will to a smaller will become little. Whoever abandons it to the will of God becomes great.

5 Magnetized by Eternal Love

S t. Edith Stein, the German-Jewish philosopher and mystic, wrote, "My impression of 'little Thérèse' was that here a human life had been worked out to the last detail purely and simply by God's love. I don't know anything greater than this, and I would like to pour as much of it as possible into my life and into the lives of those who are near to me."[9]

Thérèse herself reveals how accurate an assessment this is.

My God, the more you want to give, the more you increase the longing. I feel in myself immeasur-able wishes, and trustingly I beg you to come take possession of me.

With these words Thérèse expresses her wish to belong entirely to God. She is totally open to the love of God; there are no obstacles within her to God's love. She is porous to his love, because of her unqualified trust. By not resisting the love of God in anything, she makes surprising discoveries:

God is much kinder than you think.

God is more loving than a mother.

For a loyally received grace he gave me a host of others as well.

Accordingly, for Thérèse God is both a father and a mother. The Dutch painter Rembrandt provides a unique testimony to this in his painting "The Return of the Prodigal Son," which dates from 1666–69. The viewer's eye falls first on the back of the Prodigal Son. The face of the Prodigal Son, who had left his father's house, spent his inheritance, and returned in poverty and desperation to ask his father to take him in, remains hidden. Rembrandt leaves the returning son's facial expression to the viewer's imagination. The light is focused on both hands of the kindly father, which rest on his son's back. Rembrandt painted countless faces and hands; in this, one of his last pictures, he painted the face and hands of God.

If you look carefully at these two hands, you will notice at once how different they are from each other. The father's left hand with its spread fingers is broad, masculine, and powerful. It gives the son a firm support. But the father's right hand is delicate and tender. It doesn't grab and doesn't hold on, but softly and comfortingly rests on the son's shoulder. It is unmistakably a mother's hand. Henri J. M. Nouwen wrote of these hands: "The Father . . . is mother as well as father. He touches the son with a masculine hand and a feminine hand. He holds, and she caresses. He confirms and she consoles. He is, indeed, God, in whom both manhood and womanhood, fatherhood and motherhood, are fully present."[10]

Thérèse was profoundly sympathetic with this idea. She believed in it, and she understood God in this sense. She knew she was always loved by God in both a fatherly and motherly way. Hence her recommendation:

Let us bathe ourselves in gold through the sun of his love.

Thérèse wants nothing else but to submit to God's attraction.

How gladly would I like to let myself be magnetized by the Lord.

In the writings of St. Thérèse we find two experiences that show how this magnetic attraction affected her and can affect us. The first made her decide always to live in the radiance of the grace of God. It sheds light and warmth on our way and gives it direction. Outside this ray of light things turn dark and cold, and God's ways disappear before our eyes:

> *In the evening at the hour when the sun seems to bathe in the immensity of the waves and send out a ray of light before it, I set off all alone with Pauline to sit on a rock. . . . For a long time I observed this ray of light, an image of grace, lighting up the path that the little ship with the charming white sails was taking. . . . Sitting alongside Pauline I made a decision never to withdraw from the sight of Jesus.*

The second experience awakened in her the intention to expose herself to the divine sun — through prayer and meditation:

> *As I bent down a little, I saw through the window [of the sick room] the setting sun. It threw its last beams on Creation so that the treetops seemed all golden. Then I told myself: what a difference between remaining in the shadows and, by contrast, exposing*

oneself to the sun of Love! Then one appears entirely golden.

These descriptions also show what "meditation" meant for Thérèse, who saw likenesses in everything. First she observed something precisely, then she let herself listen to it, and then she made a firm commitment.

~

To bring his love to us, God first makes use of the people to whom he has entrusted us. It is instructive to take a brief look at Thérèse's home. Thérèse lived in a well-off family in which her mother dominated. She was very spoiled. That strengthened her rather dark qualities, of which there was no dearth: in her young years she was self-centered, proud, and jealous:

When I noticed that Céline loved one of our teachers, I wanted to imitate her. But since I didn't know how to win the favor of people, I had no luck. Oh, what a happy inability, how much distress it spared me!

Thérèse was the "last" child in the family, a word that has many shades of meaning. Those who are last not infrequently want to be first. Thérèse in fact became the first, but she chose a path that led her to an entirely different level. She wanted to become a great saint, and on this path she could bring into play her energy, her ambition, her longing for greatness, as well as her love of God, without dividing her attention.

She was first swept up into God through the goodness that she experienced in her home. Her parents were on good terms with each other and could offer their children security. She experienced something altogether different from a girl of the same age whose first item on her Christmas list was: "I wish you wouldn't always fight with each other."

But Thérèse had negatives experiences, too, and learned over and over again that God can transform negative experiences into positive ones:

My sensitive and loving heart would have easily surrendered if it had found a heart that was capable of understanding it. . . . I looked for friendship with girls my age, above all with two of them. I loved them, and for their part they loved me as far as they could. But how narrow and changeable the heart of creatures is. . . . Early on I learned that my love wasn't understood. One of my friends had to go back home and didn't return until some months later. During her absence I had thought of her and carefully kept a little ring that she had given me. When I saw my companion again, my joy was great. But what a disappointment! I got only an indifferent look from her. . . . My love hadn't been understood; I felt it, and I didn't beg for affection that I was denied. Nevertheless, God gave me such a loyal heart that it always loves once it has been loved authentically. . . . How grateful I am to Jesus that he let me find only bitterness in the friendships of this world. With a heart like mine I would have trapped myself and let my wings be clipped. Then how would it have ever been possible for me to fly and to rest?

Thérèse had several such disappointments. They were very important to her:

Who on earth knows us perfectly, and by whom are we perfectly loved?

How true it is that God alone knows the abyss of the human heart. . . . How brief are the thoughts of human beings?

How often our dear father explained to us: "God never lets himself be outdone in magnanimity."

How great must a soul have to be to embrace a God!

Thérèse, who wanted to be the prisoner of God's love, now says:

Triune God, you are the prisoner of my love.

II

THE GREATNESS OF THE "LITTLE WAY"

6 You Sustain the Universe and You Think of Me

The noted philosopher Max Scheler taught at the University of Cologne from 1919 to 1928. It was said of him by Walter Nigg that "the Cologne philosopher was a man without a firm character, a person full of seething unrest, who let himself be driven along and never got a grip on himself. His foolish wish to study decadence... came to haunt him. He wasn't up to the storms of life, and they drove him far from Christianity. Scheler himself glossed over his failure with the witty remark that 'you couldn't insist that someone who points the way should actually take it himself.' " [11]

A philosopher may talk like that, but not a saint. The saints are distinguished precisely by the fact that above all they "walk the walk" and thereby become signposts for others. The path that a saint points out is a way of life in the real sense.

The life of Saint Thérèse is a perfect example. She became world-famous precisely through her so-called "little way." She called her way "little" because anyone could take it. But we must point out something to which

Walter Nigg, with his habitual keenness, calls our attention: "The way that she teaches only seems to be little; and anyone who called it very great would not be engaging in sleight-of-hand. . . . With her teaching of the little way Thérèse found a new kind of holiness, which clothes heroism in the garment of inconspicuousness. A new path has opened up, and it has undreamt-of significance for modern saintliness."[12]

This "little way" of St. Thérèse is so great that Pope Pius XI, in his address at her canonization on May 17, 1925, said, "If this way were to be generally taken, how easily would human society be transformed for the better."

~

What then is the essence or distinct characteristic of the little way? Thérèse doesn't take a concept of God or idea of God as her starting point. At the beginning of her way there is, instead, an experience of God. Two experiences of God brought her to her path. She sums them up in a sentence:

You sustain the universe and give it life; and still you think of me.

The conviction that God sustains the universe grew from her natural mode of contemplation. It was nourished by her deep capacity for empathy, by which she sensed the song that is in all things:

If I don't see God, then, radiant nature, you are nothing more to me than a giant grave.

In that case death would have the last word, and our life would be nothing more than a being-unto-death. For Thérèse, by contrast, nature was a reflection of the greatness and power of God. The sea, which she saw for the first time at Trouville in 1878, and the mountains, which she came to know in Switzerland during her pilgrimage to Rome in 1887, had a lasting influence on her. The following description provides some sense of her extraordinary powers of observation:

Before we reached the "Eternal City," the goal of our pilgrimage, we had many more wonderful works to admire. First there was Switzerland with its mountains, whose tops were lost in the clouds, its lovely waterfalls, plunging down a thousand different ways, its deep valleys full of giant ferns and rosy

*heather. . . . How much good the beauties of nature,
spread out in such extravagant fullness, did my
soul! How my heart was lifted up by them to Him
who was pleased to lavish such masterpieces on
a place of exile. . . . The view of all these beauties
stirred my soul to deep thoughts. It seemed as if
I already understood how great God is and how
wonderful heaven is. . . . After seeing all that greatness
and power I will easily forget my insignificant little
concerns, for I wish to love Him alone.*

Thérèse reveals how greatly she suffered from her
problems. At the same time, she has found a way to forget one's little difficulties: by looking upon the things
that are great and beautiful. Thérèse says that in her
life she always loved what was great and beautiful. She
developed herself in that direction because she recognized in surrender to the great and the beautiful a way
to solve her problems.

Carl G. Jung shows how healing such a contemplative view is. He describes how patients have overcome
nearly insoluble problems by growing up and out of
them through the development of a new level of consciousness. In *The Secret of the Golden Blossom* he writes:

"Some higher and broader interest entered the field of vision and through this broadening of the horizon the insoluble problem lost its urgency. It wasn't logically solved in itself, but simply faded in the face of a newer and stronger direction in life."[13]

In contemplating the sea Thérèse had a similar experience:

> *I shall never forget the impression that the sea made on me, I couldn't help looking at it unceasingly. Its majesty, the thundering of its waves — it all spoke to my soul of the greatness and power of God.*

Elevated by such impressions, Thérèse learned to understand the images of the Bible: "Who has measured the waters in the hollow of his hand. . . . Behold, the nations are like a drop from a bucket, and are accounted as the dust on the scales; behold, he takes up the isles like fine dust" (Isa. 40:12, 15). "For a thousand years in thy sight are but as yesterday when it has past" (Ps. 90:4). "What is man that thou art mindful of him, and the son of man that thou dost care for him?" (Ps. 8:5).

Man and woman are nothing, and yet God bestows on them all his love through Jesus Christ. That is the assurance given by the Bible — that and only that is what the Bible seeks to proclaim. And it calls upon us to believe in this love that we cannot fathom.

~

John the Evangelist wrote: "So we know and believe the love God has for us" (1 John 4:16). If we make this profession of faith feel its truth, we will know an indescribable joy.

The life of Thérèse is a living commentary on this verse. Her entire life, her entire teaching are an expression of her faith in the love that God has for every person. For Thérèse faith explains everything, and without it nothing has an explanation. She never understood God as anything but "love."

God's love for man does not mean love for human beings in general. It means for every individual in his or her irrevocable uniqueness. Thérèse puts it this way:

As the sun sheds its light simultaneously on the cedars and on every little flower, as if it were the only one on earth, so our Lord turns to every individual as if there were nothing like him or her.

We find a lovely and vital development of this thought in Cardinal John Henry Newman: "God beholds thee individually, whoever thou art. He 'calls thee by thy name.' He sees thee, and understands thee, as He made thee. He knows what is in thee, all thy own peculiar feelings and thoughts, thy dispositions and likings, thy strength and thy weakness. He views thee in thy day of rejoicing, and thy day of sorrow. He sympathizes in thy hopes and thy temptations. He interests Himself in all thy anxieties and remembrances, all the risings and fallings of thy spirit. He has numbered the very hairs of thy head and the cubits of thy stature. He compasses thee round and bears thee in his arms; He takes thee up and sets thee down. He notes thy very countenance, whether smiling or in tears, whether healthful or sickly. He looks tenderly upon thy hands and thy feet; He hears thy voice, the beating of thy heart, and thy very breathing. Thou dost not love thyself better than He loves thee. Thou canst not shrink from pain more than He dislikes thy bearing it; and if He puts it on thee, it is as thou would put it on thyself, if thou art wise, for a greater good afterward."[14]

Thérèse always remained aware that nothing in her was suitable for drawing God's divine glance to herself, and his mercy alone did everything that was right in her.

———

We might reflect on a remark by Protestant theologian Jürgen Moltmann in *The First Freed Slaves of Creation*: " 'It is all for nothing,' says the nihilist and despairs. 'In reality nothing is in vain,' says the believer, who rejoices in grace and hopes in a new world, in which everything will be given and had for nothing."

7 In the Presence of God's Greatness One Gets Smaller and Smaller

The characteristic features of the "little way" can be summarized in the phrase, "You sustain the universe, and still you think of me!" The experience of God's infinite greatness and the experience of being infinitely loved by this God in one's nothingness, with one's nothingness, indeed on account of one's nothingness — that is where the "little way" begins for Thérèse, and it is the way to perfection and sanctification.

Thérèse goes on that way in a consistent fashion. Because God is great, her whole effort is concentrated on becoming ever smaller in his presence. This means becoming more and more a child before God. When the saint was asked what being little meant, she replied:

It means recognizing one's nothingness, waiting for everything from one's father like a little child.... Being little also means considering oneself... in no way capable of bringing anything to completion.... It means, finally, never getting discouraged by one's

mistakes, because children often fall; but they're too
small to hurt themselves when they do.

Becoming more and more a child in the presence of God means recognizing how tightly we are wrapped up in our own limitations and how little we can do to "change our spots," and then being conscious that we can expect nothing from ourselves, but everything from the boundless love of God.

Finally it means never allowing oneself to get discouraged by one's mistakes. Benedict of Nursia recommends in his Rule that we should "never despair of God's mercy" (IV, 74).

~

Penetrated to the depths of her heart by this awareness, Thérèse recklessly threw her "nothingness" into the "everything" of God's boundless love. What she wrote to her cousin Marie Guérin in a letter holds true for everyone:

Marie, if you are nothing, you must not forget that Jesus is everything. Hence you have to lose your little nothing in his infinite everything and think only about this everything, which alone is worthy of love.

In this trust Thérèse went on to the end:

Love your incapacity, and you'll derive more use from that than if you performed — borne up by grace — heroic acts in a burst of enthusiasm, which would fill you with personal satisfaction and arrogance.

When I fall, I recognize my nothingness still more, and I tell myself: What could I complete, what would become of me, if I relied on my own powers? I understand very well that St. Peter fell. He relied on himself, instead of holding on to God's power and nothing but. . . . Because Jesus wanted to make him realize his weakness, and because he was to rule the entire Church, which is full of sinners, he had to experience for himself how little a person can do without God's help.

Even if I had committed every conceivable crime, I would persevere in the same trust. I feel that an enormous number of insults would be like a drop of water falling into a hot oven.

Thérèse tells us in a very original manner how she could be so sure about this.

God surely has every conceivable perfection; but, if I may say so, he has at the same time a great weakness: He's blind! And there is one science that he doesn't know: counting. . . . If he were to look closely, and if he could count, don't you think that, with all our guilt, he would he let us drop back into nothingness? But no, his love for us makes him really blind. . . . In order to make him so blind, however, and to stop him from writing up even the smallest account, one has to know how to take him by the heart. That's where his weak spot is.

When we entrust our hearts to him unconditionally, we win his heart.

What offends Jesus, what wounds his heart is the lack of trust.

Trust works miracles.

What hope this gives to everyone! Many people are discontented with the way they've lived their lives. Believers may be worried about how they will ever pass muster in the sight of God and wish they could begin their lives over and do things differently. As the Russian dramatist Anton Chekhov wrote in one of his plays: "I often think: what if one could life over again? . . . What if the one life that you've already lived through was, so to speak, a first draft, of which the second would be the fair copy. Then every one of us, I think, would strive . . . not to . . . repeat himself. At least he would make another way of life for himself."[15]

But life can't be repeated. No step can be reversed, no decision, once made, can be overturned. Nothing of what we have said and done can be erased. It's hard for us to deal with that finality, hard to accept our lives as they have become. And if we were given the chance to live over again, what makes us so sure that we would do a better job of it? How fortunate it is that we have no need whatsoever to begin again. We need only entrust our lives as we've lived them to God's merciful love. Then we will be helped, however meaningless or empty our lives may have been.

Thérèse gives us an encouraging image of this. Christians are often chided for being nothing but zeroes. But for a zero the important thing is where it's placed. If it puts itself in front of the one, it remains a zero. But if it puts itself behind the one, then it acquires a value. Thus, let us place ourselves — like the good thief on the cross — behind the one, who for us is Jesus Christ. Then we will find a deep peace:

It is the serene and cheerful peace of the sailor as he sees the lighthouse that leads him to the harbor.

Thérèse can't help communicating her joy as she prays to God:

Radiant lighthouse of love, I know how one gets to you; I have found the mystery.

That is the mystery: losing one's nothingness in boundless trust in God's love.

8 Only in God's Presence Do We Learn Who We Really Are

The teaching of St. Thérèse has been compared to the teaching of the Apostle Paul, Thomas Aquinas, and Martin Luther. Her influence on the work of the French novelist Georges Bernanos has been noted. In his Apostolic Letter *Divini Amoris Scientia* Pope John Paul II attests that, "During the Second Vatican Council the Fathers repeatedly addressed the subject of her example and her teaching" (n. 10).

How is it possible? How could the Little Flower, an uneducated young girl, be named along with Christianity's greatest theologians? The answer is found in a passage in the Gospel of Matthew, which we will understand better when we think of Thérèse: "At that time Jesus declared, 'I thank thee, father, Lord of heaven and earth, that thou has hidden these things from the wise and understanding and revealed them to babes; yea, Father, for such was thy gracious will. All things have been delivered to me by the Father, and no one knows the Son except the Father, and no one knows the Father except the Son and any one to whom the Son chooses to reveal him'" (11:25–27).

The psychotherapist Eugen Drewermann writes of Jesus' words: "In a rush of happiness Jesus blesses God for the sort of truth that is hidden from the great and obvious only to the little ones.... Only the lowly, the 'little ones,' whose hearts have been broken, are open enough for God."[16] They know their weakness, and nonetheless they firmly trust in his love and help. Thérèse knew this.

To become little in the presence of God's infinite greatness is the first virtue of the "little way." Thérèse's self-awareness was deeply molded by it. How does one become little in the presence of God? By loving little things, because God loves them.

In her love for what is little, Thérèse stands in a long tradition of great minds. "Anyone who lives in contemplation of the depths will see the little things in great contexts," said Edith Stein. (That sentence also describes the life of Thérèse.) The same is true of a remark by Fyodor Dostoyevsky in one of his novels: "Let us begin small and bring it to great things."[17] The poet Manfred Hausmann tells of a young actor who completely flung himself into a minor role and turned it into the most important one in the play.[18]

Whoever can slight what is little has no sense of what is great either. Augustine said, "Being faithful in little things is something great. Do you want to be great? Begin with the small things." Francis de Sales said: "A somewhat nervous person once asked me what one can do for peace. I answered: begin by closing doors a bit more quietly!"[19] Drawing on these suggestions, we are invited to pray: "Lord, teach me to see what is great in what is little and leave the narrow space that surrounds me for your vast expanse."

The one-time Anglican primate Michael Ramsey sought to inspire his candidates for the priesthood along these lines. The ideal he held up before them was oriented both to the words and challenges of the New Testament and to the demands of the modern person. One need only let the following words take effect on oneself: "Consider our Lord himself. In the midst of a wide world full of vast kingdoms, with their mighty events and tragedies, he devoted himself to a little country, to little things, to individual men and women. He spent hours on a few people or a single person, a single woman. In a country where there were popular movements our Lord devoted many hours to the one Samaritan woman, the one Nicodemus, the one Martha, the one Mary, the one Lazarus, the one

Simon Peter; for the infinite value of the one (the little) is the key to Christian understanding of the many (the great)."[20]

Love for the little has nothing to do with pettiness, a peculiar feature of strict and domineering people.

~

The exercise of the virtue of "littleness" provides great help when we can't free ourselves from problems, when we overdramatize our everyday problems, when we take ourselves too seriously, when we have a hard time getting over, for example, a wrong done to us or a mistake we ourselves have done.

While the great simply move past such matters through sober reflection and the power of virtue, without lingering, and thus leave their difficulties behind them, the little ones often can't shake them off. We sometimes stand before them as if spellbound. Thérèse tells us we shouldn't continually ponder such things; we should stop staring at unpleasantness and brooding about it. Instead, we should simply think about something that does the soul good. Otherwise, our difficulties can drive us crazy. What a real-life feeling this has, and how precisely true it is for sensitive natures.

But there are also things that we cannot master with our own strength alone, that we experience often enough in everyday life. How often do we make the same mistake? How often do we struggle without winning a lasting victory? How often do we backslide into old bad habits? How much do we torment ourselves to push all the way to the top — like Sisyphus's rock — only to tumble right back down? How quickly can we lose heart and with it all striving for virtue? Thérèse responds to such challenges with a plain and simple dreamlike image:

I looked upon myself as a weak little bird who was covered only with a light down. True, it can lift its little wings; but it's not within its meager power to fly to the heights. . . . The little bird is in no way troubled. With bold devotion it perseveres and looks up to the divine sun. Sometimes, to be sure, it feels distressed by the storm. Then it has a hard time believing that there is anything apart from the clouds that surround it. But even then it holds out and catches sight of the invisible light that eludes its faith. . . . One day, this is my hope, beloved eagle: you will take your little bird and return with it to the focal point of love.

This bird has a characteristic call that the eagle can't resist: I am nothing, I have nothing, but I belong to you and I trust in that.

We, too, have a hard time believing that there is a blue sky above the dark clouds, when nothing is visible but the clouds. But as early as tomorrow things can look different.

Thérèse trusts patiently in the one God sent to the little, the weak, and the poor to rescue us from our distress, our mistakes, and our weaknesses, and to lift them up to those divine heights that we cannot reach with our own powers.

God always does great things for those who understand their littleness, their powerlessness, their wretchedness, and their futility, but who endure them, trusting in God's help. In his own good time God fulfills the wishes of the little ones — an experience Thérèse had again and again, because she bore within herself the conviction that God would not put unattainable wishes into our hearts. Listen to what she says:

I had always longed to become a saint. But when I compared myself with the saints, I kept finding that there was the same difference between them and me as between a mountain whose peak disappears into the heavens and an inconspicuous grain of sand that is ground beneath the feet of passersby. Instead of getting discouraged, I told myself: God can't inspire us with an unfulfillable wish; so despite my littleness I can strive for sainthood. It's impossible to make myself any bigger; I have to endure myself as I am, with all my inadequacies. But I want to seek the means to get to heaven on a little, entirely new way.

Thérèse wasn't disappointed by her faith in God's helping goodness. She was shown a way that surpassed everything she had imagined.

Thérèse knew very well that there aren't many people who wish to become and remain little. Why? We're too quick to believe that we are "somebody." We're too quick to see ourselves as smart, clever, and wise. But those things are obstacles on our path to God. Perhaps this is where we can begin to recognize our limits. Perhaps eventually it won't make any difference to us that others consider us a "nothing." That would be the moment when we would be closest to the all of God's love.

9 Simply Abandoning Oneself to the "God Who Has Come Down in the World"

P rotestant theologian Rudolf Schulz gave a radio talk a while ago that began: "Our language is alive. Certain turns of phrase are on everyone's lips, while other words fall out of use. If anyone should happen to use them at some point, the words would sound old-fashioned, stale. 'Humility' is one such word. Once it had a high status, but that's ancient history now. It's no longer part of the vocabulary of modern men and women. Evidently there's no need for the word 'humility,' because there may not even be such a thing as 'humility.' It has landed on the rubbish heap of outdated attitudes toward life."

The issue is serious: Is there really no longer any need for the virtue of humility? Does something like humility even exist anymore? It isn't hard to show how superficial such an idea is.

A text from Augustine, a message from long, long ago, explains what a "foundational phenomenon" humility is: "If you are planning to erect a tall building, first take care to lay a deep foundation. And whoever has such a wish and intention, the higher the building will be, the deeper he will lay the foundation. And the building — once it is erected — will soar into the heights; but whoever excavates the foundation has to descend into the ultimate depths. Thus the building too, before it soars into the heights, must be anchored in the depths; and the gables are built after the foundations are laid."[21]

This is a basic law. Its importance is demonstrated every time a skyscraper is constructed. Think of the laws of physics that are so crucial in erecting a tall building. To reach great heights, matching foundations have to be dug many stories deep. Without that kind of foundation a building could not withstand its height — it would simply collapse.

The correlation between height and foundation can be put this way: "Whoever wants to go high up has to go down deep." That holds true not just in the realm of engineering, but for every life that wants to reach the heights. The poet Goethe wrote: "The greatest human beings whom I have known and whose vision spanned heaven and earth were humble."[22] For Goethe, humility means having deep foundations. That is, no one can reach greatness unless he is rooted in the depths, unless he is humble.

———

"Whoever wants to go high up has to go down deep" applies above all to the saints. It's striking how they agree that humility is the foundation of their holiness. It comes as no surprise that truly great persons are always humble and modest. Without humility there is no human greatness, and it will be that way in the future too. If our age does not attribute importance to humility, it only shows that our age does not care about real greatness.

~

Thérèse understood humility as the second virtue of the "little way." She says:

It seems to me that humility is truth.

In order to understand what truth means to Thérèse we can think about the "little way" that we have taken so far. Truth comprises amazement, terror, and trust. Amazement is the echo of the human heart in the presence of the incomprehensible greatness of God, which is reflected in the variety, the richness, and the beauty of his creation. Terror, by contrast, is felt in the face of one's own littleness and powerlessness: "What is man that thou art mindful of him, the son of man that thou dost care for him?" (Ps. 8:4).

When we experience our littleness in the presence of God's greatness we are humbled. Our humility flows out of the firm belief that God's greatness — in the incarnation of his Son — looks after his little ones. To Thérèse, the secret of humility is to let oneself be swept up by "the God who has come down." This trust preserves us from self-contempt; it gives us confidence and with it the composure to abandon oneself to God.

A little incident reported by a sister shows how deeply Thérèse was rooted in the truth of humility, and as a result how little she could be disconcerted. "One of the old sisters couldn't understand that Sister Thérèse, young as she was, could be so occupied with the novices. She made no effort to conceal the hostility that she felt toward Sister Thérèse. One day at recreation time, she spoke woundingly, saying, among other things, that 'she needed to guide herself rather than worrying about guiding others.' From a distance I could clearly observe the scene. Thérèse's expression was clearly different from the passionate demeanor of her interlocutor; and I heard her reply: 'Ah, sister, you're perfectly right. I'm much more imperfect than you believe.' "

So what is the truth of humility? It is the acknowledgment of one's own narrow limits in the presence of the limitless God, and the abandonment of oneself to him in limitless trust. Only a boundless trust can correspond to a boundless God. Thérèse says:

I was strengthened by humiliations; hence I rejoiced every time that I was humiliated.

Through the exercise of humility Thérèse found one of the sources of her deep happiness. With every humiliation she was more deeply pressed into God's embrace. How do we get to such humility? It is found on the way to "last place," the place where the "God who has come down" is to be found. Thérèse was sure that on the way to this place there would be no traffic jams:

The one thing that is not envied is the last place. . . . No one will fight us for it.

St. John Vianney, the Curé d'Ars, once told his listeners: "Humility that loses heart is bad." Why? Because it lacks trust in God's merciful love. Humility and trust belong together. Without trust humility immediately sinks into despondency. P. Liagre writes: "Humility and trust: sometimes I'm tempted to trace the entire spirituality of St. Thérèse back to these two words."[23] On the basis of her humility she comes to the awareness of her powerlessness, weakness, and guilt. She knows that in the presence of God's greatness she is nothing. But in her joyous trust she casts this nothingness into the all of God's love. Even the worst guilt, as we have seen, couldn't hold her back.

Who is truly a humble person? The answer is: someone who is aware that he has nothing that he hasn't been given. Thérèse explains this truth with a reference to the New Testament:

The apostles were working all night without the Lord and didn't catch a single fish. But Jesus took pleasure in their work. He wanted to show them that he alone can give us something. He wanted the apostles to humble themselves, that is, to be aware that they could do nothing without him. Perhaps Jesus wouldn't have worked a miracle if Peter had caught a few fish. But he didn't have a single one. So Jesus immediately filled his net so much that it almost split apart. That is exactly Jesus' character: he gives as God, but he demands humility of heart.

Humility is the foundation of holiness.

Humility is truth.

Humility of heart is knowing that without the Lord we can do nothing.

10 Inner Riches
Can Lie Concealed
Behind Outer Poverty

The great figures of the spiritual life continually attest to the fact that happiness is not found outside, but in our innermost depths. In Søren Kierkegaard's words: "If an Arab in the wilderness suddenly found a wellspring in his tent, so that he constantly had an abundant supply of spring water, how happy he would consider himself. The same holds for a person who as a sensuous being is constantly turned outward, but suddenly turns inward and discovers that the wellspring lies within himself—and even more so if he discovers the wellspring that is the relationship to God."[24]

In his *Confessions* Augustine says: "Late have I loved you, O beauty ever ancient and yet so new; late have I loved you. Behold, you were within me and I was outside and I sought you there."

Anyone who wishes to encounter this happiness in his or her heart must become poor in the presence of God. Thérèse sees in such poverty the third virtue of the "little way." She describes what happiness one can reach if one experiences happiness in oneself. Our longing for external wealth abates to the extent that we have found God and in him happiness within ourselves. In other words, external riches often conceal a terrifying inner poverty and hopelessness.

~

Thérèse learned very early on that inner happiness was not to be found in outer wealth:

Wealth creates no happiness. . . . I have very clearly experienced that joy is not found in the things that surround us. It is found in the innermost part of the soul. One can find it just as well in a prison as in a palace. The proof of this is that in Carmel, even amid inner and outer trials, I am happier than I was in the world, where I was surrounded by the pleasant things of life and above all by the joys of my father's house.

God already gives in this life the hundred-fold in the least, as in the greatest, things to those who have left everything out of love for him.

Thérèse tells us that in order to reach this state of inner wealth and happiness, we must acquire the ability to let go, so that we may be able to give up many things, and ultimately everything:

On earth one should not cling to anything, even innocent things; for one has to go without them at the moment one least expects. The only thing that can satisfy is what is eternal.

Set your heart free from earthly cares, but above all from creatures; then you may be sure that Jesus will do the rest.

Céline writes in a letter to Thérèse:

"When I think about all I have to acquire!" Say, rather, all that I have to lose!... Jesus will fill your soul with light to the extent that you set it free from its imperfections.

"Leave," "lose," and "set free" — these words mean "let go" or "give up." In losing lies our gain. Ultimately life is about losing ourselves, our egotistical, anxious, and self-centered self:

I believe that Jesus' work during these exercises consisted in cutting me loose from everything that is not him.

Only those who let go of everything become empty, so God can fill their barns. Letting go also means not worrying about one's future:

You are worried about the future as if you had to determine it. Now I understand your inner unrest.... Everybody seeks...to find out the future.... The only ones who don't are the "poor in spirit."

This is another aspect of poverty. When we have let go of everything and have become so completely poor, when we stand one day in God's presence, we will have only our empty hands to show. Having become completely poor readied Thérèse to follow the "little way."

One senses such a deep peace, one is completely poor and can build only on God.

No joy can be compared to the one that the truly poor person enjoys in the spirit.

I have given everything away!...I run easily. I have nothing else but my only riches: to live on love.

~

Being small, humble, and poor are the virtues of the "little way." They don't accommodate the things people strive for by nature. That makes it all the more astonishing that through them one can experience the deepest happiness. Thérèse experienced this God-given happiness so intensely that she couldn't put it into words. The language of earth wasn't enough.

How is one to speak about things that even thought can hardly reproduce? How to speak about the depths that spread out in the most secret abysses of the soul!

I feel my powerlessness to reproduce the mysteries of heaven with earthly words. When I had sketched out pages and pages, I would find that I hadn't even begun....There are so many different horizons, so many nuances fanning out to infinity, only the palette of the heavenly painter after the night of this life can deliver to me the matching colors in order to paint the wonders that he unveils to the eye of my soul.

We need the language of heaven to express the riches that God grants.

III

GOD FORGETS NO ONE —
THAT IS WHY WE CAN
FORGET OURSELVES

11 Everything Is Ordained by God

Ida Friederike Görres tells us: "The soul has more than just this bright highest stratum; it also reaches into very dark regions below, into which even an adult only rarely gets a clear look. Anyone who knows his or her own soul even a little knows well how long it lasts and what profound transformations it demands for such a letting-go to be really carried out — not just intended, willed, decided, and expressed. The roots of a heart, sunken and wrapped into another, cannot be ripped out by a mere act of the will. And, no doubt, still less, the more the relationship is anchored in unlit, elementary depths of one's being."[25]

The plunging of Thérèse's nothingness into the everything of God's boundless love took place slowly and painfully. Her sister Pauline, who had become her second mother, left her in October 1882 to enter Carmel. "In the dark speechless depths of the blood all the forces of nature revolted immeasurably and irreconcilably against this theft. And the uproar in her soul became so overpowering that it found expression."[26]

Toward the end of that year, Thérèse was plagued by permanent headaches that were increasingly accompanied by trembling, weeping, violent agitation, attacks of cramps, and sensory disturbances. They were so vehement that there was serious concern for her mind and even her life: "The crises," reported her sister Léonie, "followed one another without respite."

Thérèse was pulled out of it by the smile of the Mother of God on the feast of Pentecost on May 13, 1883. In Mary she found a mother who could not be taken away from her:

I suffered greatly from this compulsive and inexplicable struggle, and in the process Marie may have suffered even more than I did. After vain attempts to make it clear to me that she was with me, she knelt with Léonie and Céline alongside my bed, then turned to the Mother of God and called with the insistence of a mother begging for the life of her child. Marie got what she desired. Since she found no help on earth, Thérèse likewise turned to her heavenly mother. She begged her with all her heart to finally have pity on her. Suddenly the holy Virgin appeared to me — beautiful, so beautiful that I have never seen anything more beautiful. Her face expressed an unspeakable kindness and tenderness. But what pressed all the way to the bottom of my heart was the charming smile of the holy Virgin. At this all my sufferings disappeared. Without any effort I lowered my eyes and saw Marie who was looking lovingly at me. She seemed moved, seemed to guess something about the grace that the Mother of God had granted me. Yes, I had her stirring prayers to thank for the grace of the smile from the Queen of Heaven. When she saw my glance riveted to the statue, she had said: "Thérèse is cured."

Many of the great saints have experienced the divine in a way that shook and terrified them. Thérèse, by contrast, was allowed to experience the Virgin in an inexpressibly mild fashion. The healing smile seemed to be present in everything that radiated from her. This liberating smile of the Mother of God enabled Thérèse to carry out the unbearable renunciation of her ego-core. She let go of herself and reached across the inner emptiness to grasp the hand of the Mother of God. It's not hard to imagine how intimately bound to Mary Thérèse felt from then on.

She is more mother than queen.

*The heart of a mother always understands her child,
even when it can only stammer.*

> *Your motherly glance
> drives away all my fears.
> It teaches me to weep,
> it teaches me joy.*

*I understood that I was her child. Hence I could
only address her by the name "Mama," because
this seemed to me still more tender than the name
"mother." With what passion I begged her to always
protect me.*

The last of Thérèse's prayers was to Mary. She wrote
the words (the last she would ever write) with a weak
hand on the back of a little picture of "Our Lady of
Victory":

*O Mary, if I were the Queen of Heaven and
you were Thérèse, then I would want to be
Thérèse, so that you might be the Queen of
Heaven!!!...September 8, 1897.*

∼

In our distress we too can find help in Mary. Since we are all in some way shattered, we may take refuge in trust of her. If we were "whole," then we wouldn't need her. Since her help consists above all in setting us free, she is considered the refuge of the sick, the troubled, and the weak.

12 If You Want to Be Happy, Forget Yourself

The healing experience of Pentecost, 1883, was not complete for Thérèse. The "complete conversion" was still to come. It took place on Christmas Eve, 1886, on the night that was also a "night of conversion" for Paul Claudel. "The occasion is so insignificant and almost laughable, that in recounting it one must be careful not to magnify it unsuitably in any way. In it we see faithfully mirrored our saint's habit of receiving and comprehending the divine in banal everyday things."[27]

Thérèse herself mentions this event twice in her writings:

I don't know how I could coddle myself with the agreeable thought of entering Carmel, since I was still so much in my infancy. God had to work a little miracle to make me grow in a moment, and he worked this miracle on the unforgettable feast of Christmas. . . . On that night when out of love for me he made himself weak and suffering, he made me strong and brave. . . . It was on December 25, 1886, when I was given the grace to outgrow childhood, in brief, the grace of my complete conversion. — We were coming home from midnight mass, where I had the happiness of receiving the strong and mighty God. When we arrived in Les Buissonnets, I was glad to fetch my shoes from the fireplace. This old custom had brought us so much joy in our childhood that Céline wanted to continue to treat me like a little child, since I was, after all, the youngest in the family. . . . But Jesus wanted to show me that I ought to set myself free from the mistakes of childhood. And he took away from me even its innocent joys. He allowed papa, who was tired out from the midnight mass, to get irritated when he saw my shoes lying by the fireplace, and to say words that cut me to the quick: "Well, thank God, this is the last year. . . . " I walked down the staircase to take off my hat. Céline, who knew how sensitive I was, saw the tears glistening in my eyes and said: "Thérèse, don't go down; It'll be too painful for you. . . . " But Thérèse was no longer the same as before. Jesus had transformed her heart. I fought back my tears and hurried down the stairs. . . .

In a moment Jesus had completed what I hadn't managed to do in ten years of struggling. He was

satisfied with my good will, which I never lacked.
Like the apostles, I could tell him, "Master we toiled
all night and took nothing" (Luke 5:5). Still more
compassionate to me than to his disciples, Jesus
himself took the net, threw it out, and pulled it back,
filled with fish. He made me a fisher of souls. I
sensed a great longing to work for the conversion of
sinners . . . Indeed, I felt love come into my heart, the
need to forget myself in order to bring joy to others,
and from then on I was happy.

Christmas night, 1886 was, in fact, decisive for my
conversion. But in order to characterize it more
precisely, I have to call it the night of my conversion.
On this blessed night . . . Jesus, who became a child
out of love for me, had the kindness to set me free from
the swaddling clothes and imperfections of childhood.
He transformed me in such a way that I didn't even
recognize myself. Without this transformation I would
have had to spend many more years in the world.
St. Teresa, who said to her daughters: "I want you to
be not women, but like strong men in everything,"
would not have wished to acknowledge me as her
child, if the Lord hadn't clothed me with his divine
power, if he himself hadn't armed me for war.

———

Christmas, 1886, saw Thérèse's victory over her own sensitivity, her breakthrough to freedom. Once again she had learned something very important for her later teaching. Liberation came not from spellbound seriousness about one's ego and its burdens and pains, but from decisive looking away — toward others in forgetfulness of oneself. Since one's little ego lives off the fear of falling short or being forgotten, it constantly feels threatened.

In the work of Romano Guardini (1885–1968) there is a passage that in its way speaks to us about the presence of the two selves within us: "One of the deepest paradoxes of life is that a person becomes himself all the more fully, the less he thinks about himself. Let's put this more precisely: there lives in us a false self and a true self. The constantly stressed 'I' is false, the 'me' that relates everything to one's own importance and success, that wants to enjoy and prevail and rule. This self covers up the real one, the truth of the person.

"To the extent that the first one disappears, the second will become free. To the extent that a person moves away from himself in selflessness, he will grow into the essential self. This does not look up to itself, but it is there. It also experiences itself — but in awareness of a freedom and openness, an indestructibility from within. The path on which a person gets rid of the false self and grows into the actual one is what the masters of the inner life call letting go.

"A saint is someone whose first self has been entirely overcome and whose second has become free. He or she is powerful without having to strain. He or she has no more desires and no fear. He or she is radiant. Around him or her things enter into their truth and order. Let's reduce it to its essence by saying: the person has become open to and, as it were, permeable to God. He or she is a 'door' through which God's power can pour into the world."[28]

That someone can look away from herself is a gift of grace that can come over a person at an hour predetermined by God. It can't be forced by anything, and yet the heart must be prepared to receive it.

God had known in short order how to get me to step out of the narrow circle in which I was spinning without knowing how I would ever manage to get out!

Having outgrown her true self, Thérèse came to herself. Up until her fourteenth year she was much too concerned with herself — whence her hypersensitivity and her incapacity to forget herself. On Christmas Eve, 1886, her morbid introversion turned into a healthy extroversion. Once a childish child, she became a childlike grown-up.

~

God's grace often makes use of trifles. In his biography of Thérèse, François Six writes: "It would have taken only a trifle and this event would not have taken place. If Thérèse had stayed a bit longer in the downstairs room where her father was lingering, he would have seen her and he wouldn't have spoken the words that 'cut her to the quick.' Had she gotten to her room a few seconds sooner, she wouldn't have heard those words spoken by her father. But then there was this nothing, this in-between, this staircase: 'I went straight down the stairs. . . .' "[29]

Everything comes from God. The saint herself came to realize this:

Now more than ever I understand that the trivial events of our life are ordained by God.

I feel this very precisely: everything comes from him.

Everything comes in the way God needs it. That this hour of conversion became a reality depended on a tiny detail. On the strength of this hour Thérèse became "the greatest saint of modern times" (Pope Pius X).

What Thérèse describes is imperative for God's hour of grace to become the reality of our lives:

He contented himself with my good will, which was never in short supply.

We who take the path of love should not think about what painful things may lie in store for us in the future. That would be a lack of trust and would amount to interfering with God's dispensations.

God has helped me and led me by the hand since my earliest childhood. . . . I rely on him. I am sure that he will give me his help till the very end.

Out of the experience of God's guidance in the past grows trust that God will lead us with a sure hand through an uncertain future.

13 God Carefully Prepares
Every Vocation

A Hassidic folktale recounts how in the city of Ropschitz the rich people whose houses stood alone or on the outskirts of town hired guards to watch over their property at night. One evening when Rabbi Naftali was walking at the edge of the forest, he met one of these guards. "Who do you work for?" he asked him. The man told him, but added the counter-question, "And who do *you* work for, Rabbi?" This question struck the rabbi like an arrow. "I don't work for anyone yet," he barely managed to mutter as he walked along in silence beside the guard. Finally the rabbi asked: "Do you want to be my servant?" "I'd be glad to, but what do I have to do?" the other man asked. "Nothing, except to remind me of the question, 'Who do you work for?' "[30]

This tale says something about what gives our life meaning. There has to be someone for whom we live, work, struggle, and sacrifice. Otherwise we don't grow out beyond ourselves. We remain stuck, we spin around ourselves, we make no progress. A meaninglessness spreads through us.

In her Christmas experience of 1886 Thérèse got a glimmer of her own vocation in the story of the calling of St. Peter. It was in this that the whole meaning and content and happiness of her life would consist — up to and beyond her death:

> *He made me a fisher of souls. I sensed a great desire to work for the conversion of sinners.... Indeed, I felt love enter my heart, the need to forget myself, to bring others joy, and from then on I was happy.*

But the Lord hadn't yet reached his goal with Thérèse. The final step still remained. Once again it was a "coincidence." On a Sunday early in the summer of 1887 she had as usual attended services in the cathedral of Lisieux. At the end of mass, when she closed her prayer book, a holy card depicting the crucified Christ slipped out from between its pages so that the only thing visible was Jesus' pierced and bleeding hand. Suddenly she became aware that the blood of her Lord was falling to the earth without being caught by human beings. With this, Thérèse was initiated into the suffering of her crucified Lord. At that moment, she made the decision of her life:

I decided to take my stand in spirit at the foot of the cross.

And so Thérèse discovered her vocation. She persevered in it; she prayed and sacrificed for men and women stricken with guilt and for priests. And God immediately gave her an opportunity to exercise her special vocation. In June 1887 a particularly bloodcurdling criminal trial had caught the attention of the newspapers. It was the "Pranzini case" — a hardened Italian criminal, a thief, receiver of stolen goods, and procurer had capped all that with the robbery and murder of a court lady, her maid, and a child on the night of March 16–17, 1887, in Paris. He was arrested when he attempted to sell the stolen jewels in Marseille. The trial lasted from July 7 to July 13 and ended with Pranzini being condemned to death. His execution by the guillotine was set for August 31. The press reported that he awaited his death with cynical obstinacy and brusquely repelled all approaches by the prison chaplain. With her gift for sympathy Thérèse grasped from the sensational gossip only this: a supremely unfortunate person with an unheard-of burden of guilt was on the point of death. And she wished to prevent the last and irrevocable disaster:

I said to God that I was quite sure that he would forgive the unfortunate Pranzini, and that I would believe this even if he didn't make his confession or give any sign of repentance — so great was the trust I had in the infinite compassion of Jesus. But I begged him for just one sign of repentance, simply for my consolation. My prayer was heard to the letter. On the day of his execution I happened upon the newspaper La Croix. *I opened it hastily, and what did I see? Pranzini had ascended the scaffold and was about to place his head in the cruel hole, when suddenly, in a burst of inspiration, he turned around and grasped the crucifix that the priest held out to him and he kissed the sacred wounds three times. Then his soul went forth to receive the merciful judgment of him who proclaims that there will be more joy in heaven over a single sinner who repents than over ninety-nine of the just who have no need of repentance.*

For the first time Thérèse experienced the power of prayer on behalf of others, which God had promised to her.

Don't you think that the great saints, when they see what they owe to the altogether little souls, will

*embrace them with an incomparable love? I am sure
that there will be wonderful and surprising affections
there. The person privileged by an apostle or a Doctor
of the Church will perhaps be a little shepherd
boy and the intimate friend of a patriarch will be a
simple child.*

*Imagine the stir in heaven when people get to know
those whom they have saved!*

Thérèse had promised before her death that her
actual mission would begin only in heaven:

*If God grants my wishes, I will spend my heaven on
earth until the end of time. Indeed, I want to spend
my heaven by doing good on earth.*

*God wouldn't have given me this wish to do good
on earth after my death if he didn't want to make it
come true.*

*In heaven God has to fulfill my wishes because on
earth I have never done my own will.*

*Thus we may be sure that we have at least one person
in heaven who loves us from the heart and stands up
for us in prayer until we too are where she is.*

———

It follows that we, too, should stand up for our others in prayer on their behalf. We should choose a person or a group of people whom we continually represent in prayer before God. All the great figures of faith encourage us to do so. One of these is Dostoyevsky, who writes in one of his novels: "What do you think someone feels who has nobody to pray for him? And so before you say your prayers at bedtime, add at the end the words: 'Have mercy, Lord, on all those who have no one to pray for them.' This prayer is surely pleasing to God and will be heard."[31]

There is a still more urgent invitation to such prayer that this great man of prayer, Dostoyevsky, recommends in *The Brothers Karamazov*: "Remember too, every day and whenever you can, repeat to yourself: 'Lord, have mercy on all who appear before Thee today.' For every hour and every moment thousands of men leave life on this earth, and their souls appear before God. And how many of them depart in solitude, unknown, sad, dejected; no one mourns for them or even knows whether they have even lived or not. And behold, from the other end of the earth perhaps, your prayer for their rest will rise up to God though you knew them not nor they you. How touching it must be to a soul standing in dread before the Lord to feel at that instant that, for him too, there is one to pray, that there is a fellow creature left on earth to love him. And God will look on you both more graciously, for if you have had so much pity on him, how much more will He have pity Who is infinitely more loving and merciful than you? And He will forgive him for your sake."[32]

Who do *you* work for? In whose service have you put your life? In the service of your little ego or in the service of God's great concerns? How much information about our life the answer to this question could give! The rabbi asked the guard: "Do you want to be my servant?" And when the man asked what he would have to do, he told him, "Nothing, except to remind me." Of what? Of the fact that one has to work for another. What gave the rabbi the idea to hire the guard as his servant? It had dawned on him how easy it is to lose ourselves in our own little needs and miss the divine connection into which we as believers have been called by God.

IV

TRUST DESPITE WEAKNESS
AND GUILT

14 There Is an Elevator
That Goes Up to Heaven

What is life? Dietrich Bonhoeffer's answer to that question is: "Ever since Jesus Christ said of himself, 'I am life' (John 14:16; 11:25) no thinking can get past this claim and the truth contained in it.... The saying of Jesus connects every thought about life to his person.... Life is not a thing, a being, a concept, but a person, and in fact a definite, unique person. He doesn't say: I *have*, but I *am* life.... Thus, life can never again be separated from the person of Jesus."[33]

This belief makes up the fullness of Thérèse's life, so it is not surprising that Jesus Christ becomes the center of her life. He fills up her entire life. He *is* her life. He lives in her, and she in him. Some passages from her writings may show what he meant to her:

Nothing can make me happy here on earth. True happiness is not to be met with there. My only peace, my only happiness, my only love, that is you, my Lord.

Creatures are too little to fill up the immeasurable void that Jesus has dug out in you. Give them no room in you.

Only Jesus reads in the depths of the soul.

He alone can fulfill my boundless wishes.

My director is Jesus.

Jesus needs neither books nor teachers in order to instruct people. He, the teacher of all teachers, instructs without the noise of words.

I never heard him speak, but I feel that he is in me. At every moment he leads me, inspires me to know what I should say or do. Precisely at the moment when I need them, I discover the rays of hope that I never saw before. Mostly they don't come at their richest during my contemplation but rather during my daily activities.

~

Probably her most intense statement about Jesus is to be found in a highly original letter:

*One (always) judges others by the yardstick of oneself.
And since the world is crazy, it logically thinks that
we are the crazy ones!...But after all we are not the
first to be treated this way. The only crime that Herod
accused Jesus of was of being crazy. And I judge as he
did...yes, it was crazy to seek out the wretched little
hearts of mortals....He, whose presence the heavens
cannot grasp!...He was crazy to come to earth, to
descend on sinners and to make them his friends,
his intimates, his fellows; he who was completely
happy with the two adorable persons of the Blessed
Trinity!...We shall never be able to commit for him
those follies that he committed for us. Our actions
don't deserve that name, for they're all too rational
and remain well beneath what our love would like
to accomplish. So the world is crazy since it doesn't
know what Jesus did to save it. It is a profiteer that
seduces human beings and leads them to wells that
have no water.*

"One always judges others by the yardstick of oneself" is a first-class finding of depth psychology. We
may think of what was going on in the hearts of those
who rose up against Stephen, as told in the Acts of the
Apostles. Before those people reached for rocks, they

cast at him their own inadequacies: the flying stones were just an expression of their inner hardening.

Jesus became a fool on account of his love. Anyone who loves him will likewise be taken for a fool in the eyes of the world. One of the oldest representations of the cross, perhaps the oldest one that we know, was scratched onto the wall of a room where the Roman emperor's bodyguards were quartered, not long after the death of Jesus. It portrays Jesus on the cross with a large ass's head. In front of this cross kneels a young Roman legionary. Beneath it is the inscription: "Alexamenos adores his God." This is pure irony. It means that a god who lets himself be crucified by human beings can only be an ass, and anyone who kneels before him is likewise an ass.

Nevertheless, our love, because it is too calculating and planned, remains far behind what love is capable of. Thérèse became aware that only unintentional fools for this love can bring us to God.

~

In her vivid way of expressing herself, Thérèse presents us with an image that is among the most famous of all those she created. Comparing herself with the truly great figures in the kingdom of God, she finds that there is the same difference between them and herself as between a mountain whose summit pierces the blanket of clouds and is lost in the heavens, and an insignificant grain of sand over which people thoughtlessly tramp. Instead of losing heart, she tells herself:

We live in a century of discoveries. One no longer takes the trouble to climb up the steps of a staircase. Among the rich the elevator has most conveniently replaced the steps.

The day she made this discovery she was overjoyed:

The elevator that is to carry me up to heaven is your arms, Jesus. I don't need to grow for that. On the contrary, I have to remain small, indeed, to become more and more so.

She writes to Abbé Bellière:

You are called to lift yourself up with the ELEVATOR of love to God and not to climb the steep stairs of fear. . . . Soon you will say with St. Augustine: "Love is the weight that draws me."[34]

Every good deed is thus comparable to the weights that raise an elevator as far up as they themselves go down. The feet that Jesus has bidden us wash are not on top but on the bottom of the body. In order to get to them one must make oneself small. But this is precisely how we become great in God's eyes. Every little good deed, however insignificant it may be, has its weight, which lifts the elevator of our life up to the heights of God and makes our heart wider and more filled with light.

What sets us free from our earthbound condition, what scatters the mist of our sadness or our depression, what makes us happy and gives our life meaning, are the inconspicuous works of love that everyday life provides so many opportunities to perform. Thérèse shows how to do it: with a friendly word when one would rather be silent, by staying patient when someone disturbs us:

A word, a loving smile are often enough to cheer up a sad soul.

If I have a lot to write on this day, I shift myself — so as to have an internally detached heart — into an attitude of mind of letting myself be disturbed. I tell myself: "I dedicate this free hour to being disturbed. I affirm it, I reckon with it. And if I am left in peace, I will thank God for it as for a grace that I hadn't counted on. That's why I am always happy!"

This means letting oneself be put upon, as the Good Samaritan did, being attentive when one could stay seated, creating order where someone has forgotten to, keeping a polite silence when one is unfairly accused or attacked, being kind to a person from whom no echo of gratitude will be heard, accepting a person who is unsympathetic, or putting up with somebody else's mistakes.

Now I understand that perfect love consists in bearing the mistakes of others.

This also means rejoicing in another's success, or putting a person's good qualities onto the scales when people talk about his mistakes.

Jesus looks not so much on the greatness of the deeds, nor on their difficulty, but rather on the love with which they are performed.

———

The least and lowest is precious in his eye....

Isolating oneself sterilizes the soul! One must immediately devote oneself to the works of compassion.

Good works draw the weight of our life downward, that is, toward what is hidden. We shall see how important the hidden life was for Thérèse.

What happiness our religion gives us, Instead of narrowing our hearts, as the world thinks, it raises them and makes them capable of loving, of loving with an almost infinite love, because, after all, it is to continue beyond this mortal life.

From now on Thérèse is concerned with only one science:

The science of love — that's the only one I want to learn.

15 Not Satisfied with Half-Measures

In the story of Thérèse's childhood there is one episode that sheds light on her entire life.

One day her sister Léonie came home with a basketful of odds and ends: dolls' dresses, scraps of fabric, and ribbons. Since she already considered herself a grown-up, she offered to let Céline and Thérèse pick out something for themselves: "I'm giving you all of it," she said. While Céline took pleasure in a little packet of ribbons, Thérèse declared: "I choose everything." With this she seized the entire basket.

This insignificant moment was destined — as Thérèse herself says — to become the epitome of her entire life:

My God, I choose everything, I don't want to be half a saint. I am not afraid of suffering for you. I fear only one thing, namely, keeping my will. Take it from me. "I choose everything that you want!"

Later she recognized that to become a saint it is necessary to suffer a great deal, strive for what is more perfect, and forget oneself.

There are many degrees of perfection, and everyone is free to do a little or a lot for the Lord. That is to choose among the sacrifices that he demands of us. Thérèse realized this and decided — as in her childhood — to choose everything. She had no intention of becoming a half-saint. She begged God to take away her stubbornness and willfulness, since she wanted to choose everything that God demanded of her. Thérèse longed to fulfil God's will; she wanted to become one with God in order to live in his reality. When we do God's will we make ourselves more sensitive to God's interests.

~

The wish grew in Thérèse "to carry out the most heroic works of all." She wanted to be a priest, a Doctor of the Church, and a martyr, but that still wasn't enough for her. She felt that the Church had a heart and that this heart was all in all, and she wanted to be the heart of the Church, burning with love. She cried out in the excess of her joy:

Finally I have found my vocation, my vocation is love.

On the day she died she could only say:

I don't regret surrendering myself to divine love.

Her last words were:

My God, I love you!

Thérèse's love for God took shape in the life of the community. She by no means had a natural talent for community. When she went to the abbey school of the Benedictine nuns in Lisieux, her companions found her quite unapproachable. She remained without friends and never got close to any of her teachers. Perhaps the problem was caused by her sharp eye, with which she saw the paltry, limited, petty, and malicious qualities in the life around her: "Her nature resisted the dullness of the atmosphere."[35] We can understand when Thérèse said of common life in the convent:

My cup [Matt. 26:39] *is community life.*

The Carmelite convent of Lisieux was founded in 1838; the building itself was completed in 1877. Thérèse entered Carmel on April 6, 1888. At that time there were twenty-six nuns living there, whose average age was forty-seven.

The environment Thérèse found there was not a good one. Wherever there are human beings, the world is present, and convents are part of the world too. The Carmel of Lisieux was an average place, neither on the upswing nor drifting into decline. Its spiritual father, Canon Delatroëtte, was a morose, perfunctory clerical type. He had no appreciation for what was blooming in Thérèse and often made tactless, unpleasant remarks. Upon Thérèse's entrance into Carmel, he told the prioress, Mother Marie de Gonzague, that she bore full responsibility if this girl failed to meet expectations.

The prioress was an unstable and morbidly jealous person. Ambitious and hungry for power, she tried to control the sisters entrusted to her care. She subjected Thérèse to many humiliations, continually taking her to task. Malicious remarks about the fifteen-year-old girl's inadequacies in the convent were the order of the day. When Thérèse had to weed the garden, the prioress described this chore as a stroll. According to René Laurentin, before her death in 1904 she confessed: "I have often offended God. I am the most guilty of the entire community. I would not count on being saved if I had not had Thérèse to intercede for me. I sense that I owe my salvation to her."

The lack of religious depth among the sisters led to lasting friction, which was triggered by spitefulness, hypersensitivity, and obsessive fault-finding. Thérèse was often enough misunderstood, despised, and ridiculed by her fellow sisters. Living with them she became familiar with something that never existed in her parents' house — the painful "guerrilla war of pinpricks."

In her biography of Thérèse, Ida Friederike Görres writes: "What she found was a crowd of very average, partly odd and eccentric, partly sick and overburdened, partly lukewarm and comfortable nuns."[36]

All people who live in any sort of closed institution (prisons, boarding schools, hospitals, monasteries), lose a healthy sense of proportion. Since there is no possibility of comparison, the force of emotional reactions tends to be disproportionate to the events that trigger them. We know that people who live under these conditions can experience powerful psychic jolts from seeing a bird on a windowsill or a bud on a flowering plant. Similarly, in the cloistered life of the religious, tiny events, insults, or signs of favoritism that outsiders would scarcely notice are easily blown far out of proportion.[37]

The question remains what a person makes of the situation in which she finds herself. Great saints like Ignatius Loyola preferred to enter an order in ruins, so that they would have a harder time than they would have had in the warmth and support of a "spiritual family."[38] The same can be said of Thérèse, though she certainly suffered from the lack of monastic discipline. But she neither played the part of the "misunderstood woman," nor did she give in to self-pity or seek consolation from her biological sisters. She did not rebel against her fate, but accepted the society of nuns — and every single sister in it — for what it was. She tried to transform the negative situation into a positive one.

Love knows how to profit from everything.

I always know how to find the means of being happy and profiting from my distress.

When the evil spirit tries to point out to me the failings of this or that sister whom I find less agreeable, then I quickly track down her good sides.

I always see the good side of things. There are people who take everything for the worst. With me it's the opposite. If I have nothing but severe suffering, if the skies are so gloomy that I can't see a bright spot, well, splendid, then I find joy in that.

Thérèse understood every unpleasant situation as a heaven-sent opportunity to ascend to God, and she was determined to take this path. She didn't think she already was a saint. "For her, sanctification was inner formation, shaping one's life in accordance with the will of God," said Walter Nigg. Her will was imparted to her in the saying of Jesus, "A new commandment I give to you, that you love one another" (John 13:34). Thérèse overcame herself in such a way that she succeeded, despite all the laws of natural sympathy, in loving even repulsive persons and in meeting them as if she felt a natural attraction to them.

A few years after her death the whole convent was unexpectedly transformed. This was the work of her shining example. It was so difficult, profound, and enduring a change that the sisters recognized it as the first and greatest miracle.

16 Don't Imitate
   the Chicken

Fairy tales and legends contain timeless wisdom. In the legend of Siegfried, who bathed in dragon's blood to make his whole body invulnerable, there was one little spot on which a leaf had fallen. It was precisely that spot that would one day become his doom. The story tells us that even the strongest person has a weak spot.

There is a one weakness that almost all men and women share: the susceptibility to flattery. Tell a pretty woman what a great wit she has, and she'll never forget the remark. Tell a fool that he's an original, and he'll give you a hug. Tell unsociable persons that there's something distinguished about their restraint, and they'll be delighted.

Whoever flatters us strokes our vanity by exaggerating or inventing something that just isn't there. But who wouldn't like that? Perhaps we notice the humbug at once. At first we break out in a smile of superiority, then we laugh at it and firmly brush it away. But the flatterer won't let us rest. We begin to wonder whether he might not be right after all, and in the end we believe him.

~

Thérèse knew all about this danger, because she wasn't invulnerable to praise and flattery — she explicitly stresses this about herself. In order to counter it, she was perfectly content that she was anything but an expert when it came to manual work, and was considered a klutz. Her companions often praised the talents of others in her presence, pointedly saying nothing about her. She accepted this failing of hers and turned it into a prayer, transforming earthly bitterness into a heavenly consolation. Like all great saints, Thérèse too was an artist at transformation: through prayer she turned her bad qualities into virtues.

When at the age of thirteen she left the abbey school of the Benedictine nuns during the second semester of 1885–86, she continued her education with a woman named Papinau, who was extremely learned and who lived with her mother, a Madame Cochain. In their living room with its antiquated furnishings Thérèse often sat in on all sorts of visits. On such days she didn't learn very much, but with her nose buried in her book she heard everything that was being said. In this way she found out that a certain lady admired her beautiful hair. Another woman asked as she was leaving who the pretty girl was. These words were especially flattering because they weren't consciously spoken in her presence. But Thérèse knew that her enormous longing could not be fulfilled with momentary flattery.

The more she went her "little way," the more she overcame her human vanity. She had many reasons for fighting off her intense ambition. The honor that human beings bestow upon us is extremely inconstant. There is a German proverb that says: "The saddle you're hoisted into today will be loaded onto your shoulder tomorrow." That was something that Jesus himself often experienced. Thérèse writes:

Human honor is like the wind. It passes over like smoke, which is quickly dissipated.

Honor often prevents us from becoming one with God:

How can a heart trapped in the love of creatures be intimately united with God? . . . I have seen so many people seduced by this deceptive light; they are like moths who burn their wings in it.

Vanity destroys poverty of spirit. But that poverty is the prerequisite for God's love lowering itself to us.

Let's remain far removed from everything that glitters. Let us love our littleness. Let us love to feel nothing. Then we shall be poor in spirit; and Jesus will come to get us, no matter how far away we may be.

Truth was important to Thérèse. Where does truth lie?

In reality I am only what God thinks of me.

Thérèse longed for genuine glory, and she realized where it lay:

He showed me that true wisdom consists in wanting to go unnoticed.

Nonetheless, Thérèse did long for genuine glory. Since human fame couldn't fulfill that longing, she yearned for the glory of becoming a saint — that is, to receive her glory not from human beings but from God:

I thought that I was born for glory. And when I sought for the means to acquire it, God let me realize that my glory was not for mortal eyes to see, but that it was to consist in becoming a great saint.

She expressed her intention clearly:

I prefer to remain hidden rather than enjoy half-glory. I expect the praise I deserve only from God.

The method that Thérèse used to correct a mistaken attitude has been used by other saints as well as many great men and women. Martin Buber dramatizes it in a tale called *The Tightrope Walker:* "One time Rabbi Israel was asked by his friends: 'Tell us, how should we serve God?' Rabbi Israel answered with the following story. Two friends had been guilty of committing a crime together. Because the king loved them, he wanted to give them a chance. So he ordered a tightrope to be strung over an abyss. The two guilty men were commanded to walk cross the abyss on this rope, one after the other. Whoever succeeded would have his life spared. While the first man got to the farther side effortlessly, the other one didn't dare put his foot on the rope. 'Tell me,' he cried to his friend, 'how did you manage to overcome the abyss?' His friend called back to him: 'I don't know. When I started slipping to one side, I just leaned toward the other.' "[39]

The remedy is healing an evil by applying its opposite. Francis de Sales gives another description of this practice: "When you have to deal with a character flaw, you must resort as much as possible to practicing the contrary virtue, and connect everything to it. That way you will overcome your enemy. . . . For example, if you are inclined to pride or anger, then at every opportunity you should attune yourself to gentleness and humility, and aim your prayers and other good exercises as well in this direction."[40]

We find a similar idea in Goethe: "The easygoing person should look for seriousness and strictness, the strict person should focus on an easy and comfortable nature; the strong person should aim for sweetness, the sweet person for strength, and each one will only develop his nature all the more, the more he seems to distance himself from it."[41]

The Bible tells us this in its own way: you have lived according to the flesh, now live according to the spirit. You who live from below, now live from above.

～

Thérèse found the virtue she needed to practice to counter her intense ambition. She sought out the hidden life, the life of complete self-forgetfulness. Hiddenness and self-oblivion are two of the most important concepts in both her life and her teaching:

I long to be forgotten, and not only by humans but also by myself.

All my piety was based on the word of the prophet Isaiah: "He had no form or comeliness that we should look at him, and no beauty that we should desire him.... He was despised and rejected by men, a man of sorrows, and acquainted with grief; and as one from whom men hide their faces he was despised, and we esteemed him not" [Isa. 53:2–3].

In this context we can also understand why Thérèse chose a second title of nobility — "and of the Sacred Face." In contemplating the suffering face of Jesus she discovered the mystery of the hidden Suffering Servant of God. Since God is hidden in Jesus, many people don't find him, because the world loves what glitters. It occurred to Thérèse that to find and experience the hidden God, one must live in hiding oneself:

*In order to find something that is hidden, one
must hide oneself. Our life, therefore, has to be a
mystery. . . . The* Imitation of Christ *says: "Rather be
unknown and count for nothing. . . ." And in another
passage:*

*After one has abandoned everything, one must above
all abandon oneself.*

Inexhaustible in her creation of images to express
herself, Thérèse said that in imitating Jesus, she wanted
to be nothing but a little grain of sand, over which one
simply walks.[42]

She used other images as well to say what Jesus
taught her in his school:

*So far as possible I hide what I do and lay it out at
God's casino, without worrying whether it brings me
in anything or not.*

*I play at the casino of love. . . . I play a daring game. . . . I
don't know whether I am rich or poor. I'll check and
see later.*

Thérèse chided her sister Céline, who evidently had not
been making the same kind of progress. One day Céline

remarked on how little gratitude she received for all her efforts on behalf of the community. Thérèse told her:

Acting that way would be like imitating the chicken that as soon as it's laid an egg calls every passerby's attention to it. In the exact same way, as soon as you've done something good or carried out a selfless intention, you want the whole world to learn about it and to respect you.

A Malaysian proverb says: "Turtles lay thousands of eggs without being noticed, but when a hen lays an egg, the whole country hears about it." Let's not overlook the fact that the Christian is supposed to be imitating not the hen, but the turtle, or the hidden God:

God says to me: "Give, keep giving, without worrying about the result."

Let us give without counting. One day God will say: "Now it's my turn."

These words provide encouragement for those who are continually striving for the good without any sense of success. But they also encourage those who are concerned with goodness in a community and are sometimes tempted to give up. We want to see the fruits of our effort, even though the seeds still lie under a coat of winter snow. Who knows! We should try every now and then to recall Thérèse's words: "Give, keep on giving, without worrying about the result."

Thérèse forgot herself, but she was not forgotten by the God who looks into what is hidden. Let us go up in the elevator of love. Once we arrive at our goal, God will tell us, too: "Now it's my turn!"

17 Whoever Wants
to Be a Victor
Has to Fight

How are we to become great and broad, reverent and happy? Never by accident, and only by coming into contact with good, great, generous, and reverent — in other words, exemplary — men and women, by looking up to them, by letting ourselves catch their infectious values. Why did the little people like those introduced to us by the New Testament and Christian history suddenly become great? Because in Jesus Christ they met true greatness. Thérèse felt close to three in particular.

The Mother of God had a privileged position in her life. What seemed especially worthy of imitation in this woman were the "most ordinary virtues" that she practiced:

One can easily guess that her real life in Nazareth later on must have run along quite simply.... The holy Virgin is presented as unapproachable. But one should show that she can be imitated and that she practiced the hidden virtues.

She found a truly amiable relationship with St. Cecilia, and this, too, was not without reason:

She became my favorite saint, my personal intimate. ... Everything about her fascinated me, above all her devotion and her unlimited trust.

Joan of Arc also had a very profound and lasting influence on Thérèse's life. Joan was born in 1412 and was martyred in 1431 at the age of nineteen. As a simple peasant girl, driven on by inner voices, she hurried to the royal army in order to set France free from England. Later she was captured, put on trial, and condemned to death. On May 30, 1431, she was burned at the stake in Rouen. Thérèse admired and revered the fighter in Joan. She gave Thérèse a powerful impetus:

When I read about the patriotic deeds of the French heroines, especially about those of the venerable Joan of Arc, I had a strong desire to imitate her. I thought I sensed in myself the same ardor that animated her, the same inspiration from heaven.

Speaking of herself, Thérèse declared:

I will die with my weapon in my hand.

~

Thérèse calls our attention to something very important: true greatness always has to be fought for. That holds true in both the purely human and in the religious realm. There is no true victory without struggle:

I had a very restless nature. It didn't show, but I clearly sensed it. I can assure you that I had many struggles, and a day never went by that I didn't suffer, not a single one.

It is important, too, to remember the strange truth that what for the moment may look like defeat later can prove to be victory. So Thérèse fought:

To think that I am dying in bed! I would have liked to die in an arena.

The further you march on, the fewer battles you will have or, rather, the more easily you will win them, because you see the good side of things. Then your soul will rise up above people. It is unbelievable how in the end everything that they wanted to say to me didn't even touch me, because I had recognized the lack of solidity in human judgments.

At first my features often betrayed the struggle, but gradually this impression disappeared, and the renunciation became easy for me, even in the first moment.

If you would only make what I have made — a great effort. God never denies the first grace, which gives us the courage to act. After that the heart grows stronger, and one strides from one victory to another.

We shouldn't simply let things take their course so that we can rest. We should always struggle, even when we have no hope of winning the battle. What does success mean anyway? God demands of us that we don't give up amid the difficulties of the struggle, that we don't get discouraged.

The struggle goes on until we are on our deathbed.

~

The battleground of Thérèse's life was located inside her own heart, the same place it resides in all of us.

Reinhold Schneider, an early twentieth-century writer, said: "Every person in this world can change at least one place in this world — and that is his or her own heart." Why are we so unwilling to do it? Why are we intent on changing others instead of ourselves? Thérèse gives us the answer:

The most exhausting work of all is the work on ourselves, so as to get to the point of overcoming ourselves.

The following words by Dostoyevsky support that idea: "In today's world unbridled behavior is taken for freedom, while real freedom lies only in overcoming oneself and one's will, so that one at last reaches a moral condition where one is always, at every moment, master of oneself. Unrestrained wishes lead only to slavery." In an earlier passage we read: "Only through work and struggle can we acquire independence and the feeling of self-worth. If we achieve this, we ourselves will be better, and with us our surroundings will become better too."[43]

Thérèse didn't shy away from the struggle in her own heart:

I have gone to war against myself in the realm of the spirit.

The struggle, as Thérèse explains, is against the cunning of one's own nature.

I couldn't... describe these sad stirrings of nature so well if I hadn't felt them in my own heart.

Who hasn't felt these stirrings? It's not hard for us to say unkind things about others. But once we learn that others have spoken unkindly about us, then we get annoyed and we do — as we put it — what we have to do. By words or deeds we try, consciously or unconsciously, to put ourselves at center stage. How often we think we have to say: "I have to have that!" What happens inside us when others are doing better than we are, when what they've accomplished is judged more favorably than our work?

These are the stirrings Thérèse means when she talks about the "cunning of one's own nature."

Thérèse took up the struggle against it. In the process, she discovered how much the teaching of Jesus runs counter to the stirrings of our nature. Without grace, then, it is impossible to translate his teaching into action. But with God's help Thérèse endeavored to achieve absolute control over her actions, to be their mistress and not their slave. Barely two months before her death she wrote:

The grace that went to work in my soul has to a large extent won the mastery over nature.

18 A Person's Strength
Lies in Prayer

T here are many kingdoms in this world. They are all
secured by frontiers, and the weak spots are kept
under special guard. Within us, however, there is an
entirely different kingdom, the kingdom of God, the
world of God that Jesus has opened in us:

I know and found have from experience:
"The kingdom of God is within you."

An old story recounts how Meister Eckhart prayed
for years to meet someone in whom the world of God
had dawned. One day his wish came true: in front of a
church he found a beggar in torn and shabby clothes
that were hardly worth a few farthings.

Meister Eckhart greeted the beggar with the words:
"God give you a good day, brother!" "I never had a
bad one," the man replied. In astonishment the Master asked how that was possible. The beggar told him:
"I have learned to live in God's presence. If it rains or
snows, if I am cold or if the weather is fine, then I thank

God for it, and so it's a good day. Whatever he sends me, whether joy or pain, I accept, because I know it's the best for me. So I never know unhappiness."

"Who are you really?" Meister Eckhart asked him, and again, to the Master's wonder, the beggar replied: "I am a king!" "And where is your kingdom?" "My kingdom is my soul. It is greater than any kingdom on earth." "How did you achieve this perfection?" "I have left everything to God. So I have found complete peace in him, inner joy, and eternal peace. What kingdom could be compared with that?"[44]

This story shows us what it's like to live in the kingdom of God, which is within us: the kingdom of truth and bliss, of rest, of joy, and of peace. But even in this kingdom the powers of darkness try to break in. And these powers have their own tactics. Naturally, Thérèse had no intention of getting involved with the machinations of the powers of darkness. She knew her weak points, and so she was especially vigilant about them. We, too, have to be watchful because those powers attack suddenly and unexpectedly. We have to be sober, because they intoxicate us and thus take away our levelheadedness, perceptiveness, and clarity.

This is how Thérèse fought the evil enemy:

I turn my back to the enemy, without dignifying him with a look.

One must despise all the temptations and pay no attention to them.

In her book The Master, the Monks, and Myself, Gerta Ital speaks about the necessity of "thought-control": "That's easily written... but doing it isn't easy; for if one wants to have success, this work on oneself has to be rigorous. Half-measures lead to nothing. One must become, so to speak, one's own watchdog, who immediately starts barking when something suspicious stirs.... Life will not fail to constantly put a person to the test."[45] It is necessary to have a firm, decided will:

The powers of the Evil One say: "We achieve everything, only there is this dog of good will. We can never overpower him!"

~

As different as our weak points may be, the weapons that we have to use to prevent the power of evil from breaking in are the same. The most important weapon for Thérèse was prayer. By prayer we mean "being-in-the-Lord," staying in touch with the source of light and life. Through this sort of prayer we remain lighthouses for others:

It's prayer and sacrifice that constitute my strength. Those are the unconquerable weapons that Jesus has given me. They, rather than words, can strike the soul. I have very often had this experience.

I feel that it was better to speak with God than about him; because so much self-love gets mixed up in spiritual conversations.

Prayer and sacrifice are mentioned in the same breath, perhaps because prayer is itself a sacrifice. When we pray, we have to let go of what we are doing at the moment:

Prayer is the good Lord's time. One must not take it away from him.

At prayer time God carries out his operations in us. Teresa of Ávila says: "The great mystery of prayer consists in letting God take over." During prayer, God wants to do something to us. We should leave this time to him, even if our heart is dry, even when we are overcome with fatigue. We practice endurance in fidelity:

I should be inconsolable over the fact (since the age of seven) that I fall asleep during my meditations and thanksgiving. Well, it doesn't trouble me.... I think that the little children please their parents just as much when they're asleep as when they're awake. I also think about the fact that doctors put their patients to sleep when they operate on them. Finally, I think: "The Lord knows our frailty and remembers that we are dust."

The positive thinking of the saints resounds in these lines. Thérèse took part in common prayer even when she was very sick. She thought the others would notice (and come to her aid) if she passed out.

∼

For Thérèse, prayer was the lifting of the heart above the passing world. In prayer we make our transitory life eternal by touching the eternal being of God:

How great our soul is. Let us raise it above all that is passing.... Farther up the air is so pure.

For me prayer is simply looking up to heaven.... In brief, it is something great, something supernatural, that expands my soul.

In all this, it is by no means necessary to read a beautiful prayer formulated for the particular situation from a book, in order to get a hearing.... Apart from the divine office, which I am very unworthy to pray, I don't have the courage to force myself to seek out such prayers in books. That gives me a headache. There are so many of them... and each one is more beautiful than the next.... I couldn't pray them all, and since I don't know which one to choose, I do what children do who can't read. I simply tell the good Lord what I want to tell him, without beautiful phrases, and He always understands me.

Simple prayer was the most helpful kind for Thérèse. Simple prayer comes from inside ourselves. We pick up any stimulus, think it over, and try to come closer to God in intimate acts of faith and love. Thérèse disliked hasty and wordy prayers:

———

*When my mind finds itself in such great dryness
that it is impossible for me to pull a thought out of
it to unite myself with God, then I pray very slowly
an Our Father and then the Angelus. These prayers
give me wings. They supply my soul with far more
nourishment than if I had plunged ahead and reeled
them off a hundred times in a row.*

*Our Father in heaven. How consoling this phrase is.
What an infinite horizon it opens up to out eyes.*

Along with simple prayer Thérèse knew many different forms of interior prayer. She knew prayer as a loving act of lingering with God. Her sister Céline tells us: "Against her wishes I often got up in the night to check up on her. Once I found my sister with hands folded and eyes directed to heaven, 'What are you doing?' I asked her. 'You should try to sleep!' 'I can't. I'm suffering too much. So I'm praying. . . . ' 'And what do you say to Jesus?' 'I tell him nothing. I love him!' "

She knew prayer as the gaze of the contemplative: "Videntes videre."[46] She looked into the eyes of the Crucified and had silent conversation with him: "Your face is my only riches," says one of her poems. Such loving "being-with-the-Lord" was to her mind the highest form of prayer.

Beyond that, Thérèse speaks of prayer as the opportunity to lose oneself in God. In that way our finite being loses itself in infinity:

I had vanished as the drop of water loses itself in the ocean.

For Thérèse prayer didn't only mean becoming one with God; it also meant speaking up for others in God's presence:

Becoming an apostle of the apostles through prayer and sacrifice.

As others owe us a great deal for our prayers, so we owe a great deal to the prayers of others, who often enough remain unknown to us and hidden from us. For Thérèse prayer was the lever that turns the world upside down:

A learned man once said: "Give me a lever, a place to stand on, and I will move the world." What Archimedes couldn't accomplish . . . the saints achieved in all its fullness. The Almighty gave them as a base GOD HIMSELF and as a lever GOD ALONE: prayer, and in this way they turned the world upside down, and in this way the militant saints today turn it upside down, and till the end of the world the future saints will do likewise.

V

GETTING TO KNOW
GOD'S CHARACTER

19 Those Who Plunge into the Bible Get to Know God's Character

I t is hard to imagine world history without thinking of a host of significant men and women, among them the ancient Greek philosopher Socrates. His mother was a midwife, his father a sculptor. From both his parents he learned to bring hidden treasures to light. Socrates believed that there is much good in every person but that it has to be lifted out and addressed. This was the essence of Socrates' dedication to his fellow humans.

Doesn't this belief still speak to us today? We often refuse to trust this Socratic wisdom. We ignore people, show no interest in them, and because we don't take the trouble to get to know them and to bring out their inner riches, we ourselves remain spiritually poor. Eugen Roth once wrote a poem that can serve as a starting point for the renewal of our relationships with people — indeed, for the renewal of the life of our entire community.

A person may be ever so worthless —
he's still not just a dumb stone:
even if he doesn't exactly have a heart of gold,
everyone bears a little ore:
whether silver, copper, iron, or tin,
even if it's just lead,
there's something in there.
But nobody, though we should,
bothers to dig deeper,
because we insist in advance
that mining there likely isn't worth it.[47]

How rich a community would be if its members were thought of as "mines" where precious treasures had been hidden — above all, if we were to see this from a religious perspective. Is there any one of us whom God hasn't richly blessed in some way or another? There is the idea, too, that it is God's providence that has led every individual to a specific family or community.

~

There is not just a human providence, but a "book providence," which, according to Ida F. Görres, "in the most amazing fashion often thrusts the right book into our hands at the right moment (since every book that's important for us has its moment)." A book with an appealing content can awaken riches that are slumbering in us and give us a decisive stimulus, a push that flings open the door to a whole new world.

How did "book providence" work out in the life of Thérèse? She liked to read, and she said that while she was reading she forgot time. As a young girl she loved chivalric romances. This is how she came to know the life of Joan of Arc. Thérèse's noble, aristocratic, and "knightly" qualities, as well as her courage to fight, found nourishment there.

The "bread" of her life soon became *The Imitation of Christ* by Thomas à Kempis, which she knew by heart. At the time she read it this book was the only one that did her soul good. Ida Görres writes: "Thomas à Kempis is decidedly old-style wisdom, the final harvest of a soul that is thoroughly mature and has become quiet, having outgrown all fantasy and brooding, far removed from all dreams and disappointments. This wisdom-turned-simplicity has created its own language, so quiet and spare, so careful and precise, that a young person, a beginner, is likely to skim over it in frustration, as if it were just commonplaces and hoary old truths."[48]

Another book that provided her with "honey and oil" was the lectures of a certain Abbé Arminjon, *On the End of the World and the Mysteries of the Future Life*, a volume that can no longer be found anywhere. The Carmelite sisters had lent it to her father, and it became Thérèse's regular reading. While she went to Thomas à Kempis's school of wisdom and simplicity, Abbé Arminjon's book instilled in her an insatiable longing for heaven.

At ages seventeen and eighteen she drew most of her spiritual nourishment from the writings of St. John of the Cross. She received much spiritual enlightenment from them. By occupying herself with this great mystic from her own order she found her way to the Bible.

The Bible gave Thérèse immediate contact with God. She gave up all other books to dedicate herself to the study of Scripture. She read the Bible to get to know God, to discover his character, as it were. Above all, the Gospels gave her what she needed for inner prayer. The variants in the translations greatly troubled her, and she would have very much liked to study Hebrew and Greek so she could read the word of God in the original. Thérèse says about Holy Scripture:

Sometimes when I read certain religious treatises, in which perfection is described as . . . passing through

all sorts of difficulties, my mind gets tired very
quickly. I close the learned book... and reach for
Holy Scripture. Then everything seems to me full of
light. A single word opens up infinite horizons to me.
Perfection seems easy to me. I see that it is enough
to recognize one's nothingness and to throw oneself
like a child into God's arms.

Like Dostoyevsky, Thérèse had a believer's conviction
that there is a "biblical providence." In Dostoyevsky's
novel The Possessed, Sofya Matveyevna reads from the
Bible to Stepan Trofimovich, who is lying sick in bed.
After a brief interruption Stepan says: "Read me some
more, open the book at random and read the first thing
that strikes your eye." Sofya opens the book and tries
to begin. "Where it opens by itself," he repeats, "where
it opens by itself."[49]

Dostoyevsky was still practicing "biblical providence"
on the day he died. He told his wife, "I know I have
to die today." She tried to calm him down, but he
answered, "Give me the Gospel."

The edition he asked for had been his trusted advisor
for many years. When he was in doubt about anything
and couldn't reach a decision, he opened the Bible and
read whatever he found on the left-hand page. He did

the same thing on the day he died. He opened the book and asked his wife to read it out to him. She read from the Gospel of Matthew 3:14–15: "John would have prevented him, saying, 'I need to be baptized by you, and do you come to me?' But Jesus answered him, 'Let it be so now.'" "Do you hear?" Dostoyevsky said. "Let it be so now! Therefore, I am dying." He closed the book. At around 8:30 that evening he entered God's eternity.[50]

Thérèse too loved taking random dips into the Bible. When she did, she expected that the verse her eye first happened on would be one that God had led her to in order to solve a problem or shed light on a doubt.[51]

> *I immediately felt the urge to open the Gospel. And as I opened it at random, my glance fell on a passage that I had never noticed before.*[52]

A passage at the very beginning of Thérèse's *Autobiographical Writings* reflects on the mystery of her vocation:

> *When I opened the Holy Gospel then, my eyes fell on the words: "And he went up on the mountain and called to him those whom he desired; and they came to him" (Mark 3:13). Here it is, the mystery of my*

vocation, of my entire life.... He doesn't call those who are worthy, but those whom he wants to call.

For the believing Christian the preaching of the Gospel at a Eucharistic service is something like a random dip into the Bible done on our behalf. The moment when the Good News is proclaimed should be one of the most important moments of our day. Internally open, we should listen for the word that God wants to speak to us on this specific day.

Thérèse also read the Bible systematically. She greatly loved the prophet Isaiah. She had read fifty chapters in the book without feeling touched by any verse in a special way. But then she suddenly and unexpectedly found in chapter 53 or 66 the words that gave her crucial help in proceeding on her way. At such moments she rejoiced like the woman in the Gospel who finally recovers the drachma she has lost (Luke 15:18).

When she experienced something she often connected the experience to a familiar saying in the Bible. When the holy picture fell out of her prayer book and she intuitively grasped her vocation for compassion, she realized what the Lord's thirst meant and immediately recalled the saying of Jesus on the cross, "I thirst" (John 19:28).

Two passages from her writings show how original Thérèse was in her reading of the Bible:

Let us hear what he tells us: "Make haste and come down, for I must stay at your house today" (Luke 19:5). But where are we to climb down to? Once the Jews asked: "Rabbi, Where are you staying?" (John 1:39). And he answered them: "Foxes have holes, and birds of the air have nests; but the Son of man has nowhere to lay his head" (Matt. 8:20). That is where we must climb down to, so that we can serve Jesus as his dwelling. Jesus wants us to receive him in our heart (now empty and poor). Unfortunately, I feel that mine is not quite empty of myself. That is why Jesus tells me I should climb down — climb down into my heart, in order to make it empty of myself, so that he can stay in it.

What if people don't understand us and judge us unfavorably, and then we defend ourselves or try to explain ourselves? Let's just let it be and say nothing. It's so good to say nothing, to let oneself be judged, regardless of how. In the Gospel we find no trace of Mary's justifying herself when her sister condemned her for sitting at Jesus' feet without doing anything.

She never said: "Martha, if you could imagine the happiness I feel, if you were to hear the words that I'm hearing.... And besides, it's Jesus who asked me to stay here." No, she prefers to be silent. Happy silence, which gives the soul such peace.

20 The Teaching of the "Little Way" in Suffering's Trial by Fire

Goethe once remarked, "When a person can no longer become something different, then he shows who he is." This is as true as it is laconic. Goethe means that the real state of affairs in someone's inner life is revealed in the hours of fateful trials, the moments when difficulty arises — a serious sickness or an all-engulfing pain. Such hours are moments of truth. Sometimes we can only stare in amazement at what human greatness comes to light in such times. This is the case with Thérèse.

The life of St. Thérèse, especially as it drew to its close, was engulfed in pain. She was twenty-three years old when she was struck with the galloping consumption that asphyxiated her a year and a half later after a severe death agony.

In addition, around the turn of the century the methods of handling her disease were not exactly gentle. Her sister Céline, who was her nurse, writes: "I can still see her as she was being jabbed more than five hundred

times with a red-hot needle (I counted them precisely)."
Thérèse tells how she felt during her fatal illness:

What a grace to have faith. If I didn't have faith, I would have committed suicide without hesitation.

I understand very well why those who don't have faith take their lives when they suffer like this.

I'm amazed that among the atheists there aren't more people who take their own lives.

Along with her bodily sufferings (if the term "bodily" can be applied to the body alone) went her mental ones. They were triggered when her father, whom she loved very much, became increasingly deranged. His condition worsened to the point that he had to be put in a nursing home, where he lived for three years. He died in 1894.

In our dear father Jesus has struck the most sensitive outer part of our heart.

Thérèse found the nasty talk of people more painful than five hundred needles. The most painful suffering she had to endure was being plunged into the night of nothingness:

God tests us in what is dearest to us.

She felt like she was in a dark tunnel where she could see absolutely nothing. She was standing in front of a wall that reached up to heaven and blocked out everything. A massive doubt about eternal life swept over her and called her entire religious life into question:

Once I couldn't imagine that there really are godless people, people who have no faith. I always thought that they were speaking against their better knowledge when they denied the existence of God.... But Jesus let me feel that there really are people without faith.... He allowed the thickest darkness to penetrate my soul. And the precious thought of heaven was now just an occasion for struggle and torment.... You have to have walked through this dark tunnel to know just how black it is.

In situations like this the only thing she had left was the inscrutable word of God, and she staked everything on that word. Biblical faith in the actual sense only begins when one has nothing left but God's word, which appears to be fully absurd in every way. Thérèse was the companion in destiny of all those burdened by severe mental suffering and all those who live without hope and find life meaningless.

Today a statue of Thérèse stands on the pediment of the basilica built in her honor, a symbolic way of saying that she reached the heights on her "little way." How was she able to take this path, to go from depth to height, from darkness into light? The answer, which is important for all of us, is found in one of her letters:

The little crosses are all my joy. They are more an everyday affair than the heavy ones, and they prepare our heart to accept the latter when our Good Master wills it.

The acceptance of recurring unpleasantness, inconsistencies, worries, and daily strains, of situations where one has to make little acts of renunciation: these are the little crosses through which the power to take on the great crosses grows in us. Thérèse says:

A day that has passed without sacrifice is a lost day.

Thérèse admits that she didn't always feel that way:

Earlier, when I still lived in "the world," when I woke up in the morning, I thought about what would probably happen to me in the course of the day. And if I anticipated only disagreeable things, then I got up all depressed. Today it's exactly the opposite.... I feel all the more cheerful and bold insofar as I foresee several opportunities to prove my love to Jesus.

Her inner attitude toward difficulties and pain had changed. If earlier she had suffered in sadness, now she suffered in love:

Suffering stretched out its arms to me, and I threw myself lovingly into them.

Although Thérèse learned to accept pain in love by taking on the many little crosses of everyday life, there was another way she acquired her great capacity for suffering. She regularly made the Stations of the Cross, station by station. She saw through Jesus' example what could be done in the face of suffering, guilt, and death. She saw the Lord praying in the garden of Gethsemani on the night before his crucifixion, and she learned how to renounce her own will. She saw how Jesus was taken prisoner, and she learned to surrender her freedom. She saw how Jesus was interrogated, and she learned not to insist on her rights. She saw how Jesus was scourged, and she realized that it is not the healthy, robust one, but the vulnerable one, who is the real person. She saw how Jesus was mocked, and she learned to endure loneliness. She saw Jesus bear his cross, and she learned that the story of Jesus is the story of our own lives.

In this way Thérèse gave her own life meaning. She suffered as a representative of all those who work in the kingdom of God, of all those who find themselves in the darkness of guilt and who shy away from the light, of all those who live in the night of unbelief. She accepted suffering in love in order to suffer through it — as Jesus did in the presence of God as a representative of others. The mystery of her suffering has to become the mystery of our own lives. When it does, we will have extraordinary experiences through the suffering we have accepted.

Thérèse tells us what these experiences are like:

When one loves something, the pain disappears.
[Augustine] [53]

I have often noticed that it makes one kind and considerate to other people when one has to bear suffering.

God gives me exactly what I can bear.

I have no fear; God will give me the strength. He doesn't leave me in the lurch.

Whereas during my childhood I suffered in sadness, now I don't suffer that way anymore, but in joy and peace. I am really happy to suffer.

I have gotten used to always accepting suffering amiably.

God alone must be enough for us when it pleases him to pull away the branch that bore the little bird. The bird has wings; it's made for flying.

The three years of papa's martyrdom seemed to me the dearest and most fruitful of all our lives. I wouldn't exchange them for all the ecstasies of the saints.

Suffering lovingly, that is the purest happiness.

Thérèse's words remind me of the impression I had when I saw the monument to the Roman empress Gallia

Placidia in Ravenna. From the outside, it's not a handsome structure. But once I entered it, I felt as if a heaven on earth had opened up to me. It can also be that way with suffering. Viewed from the outside, it has a negative effect on us. But if we accept it in love, it will let us sense something of the glory of God.

21 Life Is a Continuous Parting

Everything that has a beginning sooner or later has an end. This is normal and doesn't strike anyone as unusual, as long as this law doesn't get under our own skin and make us realize that it unmistakably applies to us too. As soon as we notice that our own life will end, we are hard-pressed to deal with it. For obvious as it is that every life will one day come to a close, we can hardly imagine that some day we will no longer be in the world and that everything will go on as if nothing had happened. But that's exactly how it's going to be. Every day that comes to an end reminds us of this fact.

What is life? This is a question that Thérèse repeatedly asked herself. When she had had a Sunday full of experiences, when the holidays came to an end, when the last day of the year arrived, in hours when she had to say goodbye to someone who was dear to her, she posed the question, What is life? In her *Autobiographical Writings* we read:

In a moment I grasped what life is.... I saw that it is... a continuous parting.

Thérèse felt that life was an ongoing process of saying goodbye. How often we have to say goodbye, to school, to our parents' house, to the individual stages of life, to friends, to countries where we may have gone on vacation. Ernst Wiechert, a contemporary writer, imagines a long rack in a large room. On the rack hang all the suits or dresses that we have worn thus far. Beneath it are our shoes. They all call out to us soundlessly but urgently: "Life is a constant separation, an ongoing farewell." The French popular singer Mireille Matthieu sang, "Part of life is saying goodbye, part of life is the word 'adieu.'"

～

It's not hard to say why bidding farewell causes problems. The place where one has lived is familiar. One has come to know one's surroundings and gotten used to the people there. Bonds have been created. All that imparts a feeling of security and quiet happiness.

It is remarkable that one often becomes aware of such feelings only in the moment of going away. Goethe said that only at partings do we feel what the busy moments have hidden in silence. Only when we say goodbye does life show its deeper, more painful reality. Perhaps all suffering is essentially a kind of parting. That's how it felt to Thérèse.

With every farewell we become aware of impermanence and with that the preciousness of our earthly existence. Without goodbyes, we would fall prey to laziness, which is one of life's greatest enemies. In his poem "Life's Stages," Hermann Hesse says: "Go on then, heart; say goodbye and be cured." Above all, say goodbye to what isn't good for you, to what makes you small and keeps you small. Say goodbye to bad qualities, to all that takes away breadth and dignity.

In moments of farewell we realize that everything in life is a gift. When I was working in a parish in Westphalia, I met parents who had just tragically lost three daughters in the bloom of their youth. The father, laying the whole weight of his sorrow-tested heart in his words, said, "We thank God for the years when we were allowed to have our daughters." This is the "gratitude in tears" that Søren Kierkegaard once spoke of. It is the most profound answer that can be given to life. It guards us from bitterness when the moment comes for us to say adieu.

There is another reason why God continually makes us say farewell. He wants us to be ready to set off and to remain ready until the end. Setting off means daring to head out into what is unfamiliar, unknown, and uncertain, so life becomes a journey of discovery. The only people who really live are those who can bid farewell. Thérèse made her own a line by a French poet:

> Life is your ship,
> it's not your home.

Our life is only a transitional phase, and to Thérèse:

We are travelers on our way to an eternal homeland.

Life has a goal. Psychoanalysis finds that there is a powerful unconscious drive in our personality urging us to accept that life continues after death. Our longing for immortality is a basic part of the structure of our being. Thérèse says:

In the depths of our heart we sense that there is an eternal day.

Anyone who believes that life goes on after death is following the drive of his or her unconscious. By contrast, anyone who declares that he or she does not believe in it is rejecting one of the deepest longings of the human person. It is self-evident that this rejection exacts a high price in psychic energy.

The experience of continuous separation and the awareness that our life is only a transitional phase leads the saint to say:

How good it feels to think that we are on the way to the eternal shores.

Thérèse believes that Jesus is the pilot of the ship of her life. And she is sure that he will reach the harbor of eternity on the day that is best for us. Jesus is with us, in the boat, even when we think that he is far away.

~

In the lives of the saints and in our own lives as well there is an experience out of which emerges another answer to the question, "What is life?":

How little I have lived. Life always seemed very short to me. It seems as if the days of my childhood were only yesterday.

All of us have experienced the feeling that with increasing age one's lifetime passes away even more quickly. In childhood a year seemed to last forever, but in middle age we have the impression that time is flying. The older a person gets, the more he or she imagines life compressed into a brief moment:

> Let us look at life in its true light. . . . It is a moment between two eternities.

The quickness with which our life seems to pass can lead to important resolutions:

> Let's use the brief moment of our life. . . .

> One should cling to nothing on earth. . . . The only thing that can satisfy us is what is eternal.

> This thought of the brief time of life gives me courage and helps me to bear the labors of the way.

The words of the Apostle Paul are apt: "I consider that the sufferings of this present time are not worth comparing with the glory that is to be revealed to us" (Rom. 8:18). With increasing years the mystery of our life becomes greater, not smaller.

———

Henri Lacordaire (1802–62), the great French Dominican preacher, declared at the moment of his death: "I am tremendously curious." Or, to put it another way, the best always lies before us.

22 "I Feel That There Is a Heaven"

I n *The Brothers Karamazov* Dostoyevsky's *starets* (elder) Father Zosima says, "Instead of the boiling blood [of youth] there comes the rest of gentle, clear age. I still rejoice at the daily rising of the sun, but now I love its setting even more. My life is coming to an end; I know it and feel it. But I also feel with each declining day that my earthly life is in contact with a new, unending, unknown, but approaching life, and in my presentiment of it my heart trembles with joy."[54] All of us can understand that feeling in some way.

In the writings of St. Thérèse we note the recurring phrase, "Je sens," or "I feel." She writes:

I feel that there is a heaven, and that this heaven is populated with men and women who love me. . . .

Just as the genius of Christopher Columbus made him intuit the existence of a new world when nobody else was thinking of it, so I feel that one day another earth will serve as my enduring residence.

In the refectory of the Carmelite convent a biography of Columbus had been read to the nuns. It told how Columbus refused to be put off, even when the ship's crew tried to make him give up the dangerous journey. In the same way Thérèse felt that heaven exists. And the peculiar thing about this feeling is that it is more certain and profound than any proof could be. Perhaps we find ourselves asking: How can there be a heaven and in it a kindly Father when he allows so much suffering, cruelty, natural catastrophe, and crime?

There is little we can do to answer this besetting question, but it is worth noting that the question has not yet overcome our deep feeling for God's existence and his heaven. Evidently that feeling is much deeper than our doubts, weighty as they may be. Indeed, it appears that this feeling can support the doubts.

~

It seems to me that in the lives of all of us there is something that nourishes this feeling of the existence of heaven. It is those sunny, happy moments when we think we are experiencing "heaven on earth."

I recently heard an interview on the radio in which various people were asked whether they had had such an experience. One woman described how she had gotten over a leg injury: her words almost tumbled over each other, so surprised was she to be able to walk again. A man told of being in a prison where a Russian woman gave him, a starving young man, something from her pot to eat. You could sense from his account how unforgettable this had been for him. Another woman was still overwhelmed by the experience of happiness — although it had happened twenty years before — at the birth of her child, whom she had been very worried about.

Such moments, in which one senses the presence of a completely different world, are familiar to all of us: experiences of happiness that we can hardly describe, where something happens to us to cause a joy that long reflection and pondering could never have achieved. Though the gray everyday scene immediately catches up with us, unforgettable recollections of such experiences remain behind. Still more, we have the knowledge that hanging over all the dark hours of our life there is a greater reality. We should think back on precisely these sunny moments when suffering, sickness, or disappointments pull us so far into the darkness that we could lose our faith in heaven. It is in suffering that we can lose sight of the big picture, since we see only ourselves and our momentary wretchedness. This should be a principle of life: in the dark hours of your life remain true to what you saw in the light.

Thérèse's basic feeling for the existence of heaven was nourished by fulfilling God's will:

My heart is completely filled by God's will... even when something is going on right next to me.

May God's will be done. Rest is to be found only in that.

Perfection consists in doing his will, to be what he wants us to be.

In this way, we become who we are supposed to become. Fulfilling God's will means living on the basis of the You that is God. Since Thérèse did God's will, she and God were wrapped up in each other, and she experienced heaven on earth:

Some time ago I came across a saying that I find very beautiful.... "Inspiration is still different from God's will." It's the same difference that exists between uniting and union. In uniting there are still two parties, in union only one.

Thérèse recognized God's will by living each moment and staying oblivious to worry and fear for the future:

I don't upset myself. I wish to think only of the present moment.

I suffer only from moment to moment.

From one moment to the next one can bear a great deal.

Hans Urs von Balthasar writes: "Thus Thérèse experiences in calm and cheerfulness something of what the poets and Romantic writers vainly yearned for: eternity in the completely fulfilled moment of time."[55] While Thérèse lived the concrete moment, she completely exploited the time God granted her. Translating God's will into reality led to Thérèse's self-realization.

$\sim$

How then does Thérèse describe the eternal joy and happiness of heaven?

In heaven there are no more graves.
I see what I have believed,
I possess what I hoped for,

I am united with the one whom I have loved,
with all my loving energy.

In Thomas Aquinas's words: "In heaven every one of the elect rejoices in the happiness of the others." In the book by Abbé Arminjon Thérèse had read, "Everyone will be rich through the riches of all, everyone will be gripped by the joy of all."

Thérèse describes the deepest happiness of heaven:

God will be the soul of our soul... unfathomable
mystery....

Thérèse invites all of us:

> *Let us go our way in peace,*
> *with our eyes raised to heaven,*
> *the only goal of our toils.*

Afterword

If you look up the term "Doctor of the Church" in the latest edition of the massive German *Lexikon for Theology and Church*, the entry reads: "Ever since the phrase was comprehensively defined by Benedict XIV, 'Doctors of the Church' means persons whom the Church has officially designated as notable for the holiness of their lives, their orthodox faith, and their outstanding teaching."[56] If you look through the list of the Doctors of the Church, you'll find among them names like Augustine, Thomas Aquinas, Bernard of Clairvaux, Francis de Sales, Albert the Great, Teresa of Avila, Catherine of Siena, and, at the end of the list, ever since 1997, Thérèse of Lisieux.

In the *Autobiographical Writings of Thérèse of Lisieux* the term "Doctor of the Church" is mentioned twice. On the strength of her solid knowledge of the catechism, which she studied during the breaks between classes, and on account of her namesake, Teresa of Avila, she tells us that her religion teacher called her his "little Doctor of the Church." In another passage, Thérèse writes:

I feel the vocation to be a warrior, a priest, an apostle, a Doctor of the Church, a martyr. . . . Despite my littleness I would like to enlighten people as the prophets and Doctors of the Church did. I have a calling to be an apostle.

Step by step, through a series of extraordinary strokes, this intense wish turned into a reality. It would be no exaggeration to say that once her *Autobiographical Writings* became known, Thérèse of Lisieux was unofficially recognized and revered as a Doctor of the Church.

Her official elevation to Doctor of the Church was announced by Pope John Paul II at the end of the twelfth World Youth Congress in Paris on August 24, 1997, at the recitation of the Angelus. "In response to many requests," the pope said, "and after careful study, I have the joy to announce that on Mission Sunday, October 19, 1997, at St. Peter's in Rome I shall declare St. Thérèse of the Child Jesus and of the Sacred Face a Doctor of the Church."[57]

In this context it should be mentioned that in Thérèse this pope had, from his youth, venerated a saint who deeply influenced his own life, as he stressed in his sermon at Lisieux on June 2, 1980. So it's no surprise

that John Paul II — like his twentieth-century prede-
cessors — continually emphasized the thoughts and
teaching of Thérèse in his sermons.

At the end of his extensive Apostolic Letter *Divini
Amoris Scientia* (n. 12) on the proclamation of St. Thérése
as a Doctor of the Church, the pope noted: "Today on
October 19, 1991, before a crowd of believers from all
over the world thronging St. Peter's Square, and in the
presence of many cardinals, archbishops, and bishops,
at a solemn Eucharist I proclaimed Thérèse of the Child
Jesus and the Sacred Face a Doctor of the Church." And
further: "In keeping with the wishes of a great number
of my brothers in the episcopacy and numerous believers from all over the world, after listening to the report
of the Congregation for Beatification and Canonization
Trials, and after receiving the vote of the Congregation
for the Doctrine of the Faith concerning this 'outstanding teacher,' we declare from certain knowledge and
after mature reflection, by virtue of our full apostolic
authority, St. Thérèse of the Child Jesus and the Sacred
Face a Doctor of the Church, In the name of the Father
and the Son and the Holy Spirit."

Since the pope continually points in his letter to
the importance of the teaching of St. Thérèse and

to the "universal dissemination of her message," that might make us curious to know what the teaching of this youngest and most recent Doctor of the Church actually was.

Rudolf Stertenbrink, O.P.

Notes

1. *Lexikon für Theologie und Kirche*, ed. Walter Kasper, et al., 3d ed. (Freiburg i. Br., 1991), 6:20–21.

2. World Youth Congress, Paris, August 24, 1997, n. 3.

3. Jakob J. Petuchowski, *Es lehrten unsere Meister: Rabbinische Geschichten* (Freiburg i. Br., 1979), 131–32.

4. Meister Eckhart, *Deustche Werke*, vol. 5: *Meister Eckharts Traktate*, ed. and trans. Josef Quint, Treatise 3, "Von Abgeschiedenheit" (Stuttgart, 1963), 544.

5. Søren Kierkegaard, *Erbauliche Reden*, 1850–51, GTB 622 (Gütersloh, 1995), 5.

6. A. Combes, *Die Heilige des Atomzeitalters: Thérèse von Lisieux* (Vienna and Munich, 1957), 241.

7. Hans Urs von Balthasar, "Der 'kleine Weg': Zum hundertsten Geburtstag der Thérèse von Lisieux am 2. Januar 1973," quoted in *Deutsche Tagespost*, January 5–6, 1973, 14.

8. Jörg Zink, *Sieh nach den Sternen — gib acht auf die Gassen* (Stuttgart, 1992), 72.

9. See Ida Friederike Görres, *Das Senfkorn von Lisieux* (Freiburg i. Br., 1958), 525.

10. Alois Amrein in a personal communication to the author.

11. Edith Stein, *Endliches und ewiges Sein: Versuch einer Aufstieg zum Sinn des Seins* (Freiburg i. Br., 1950), 361.

12. Henri J. M. Nouwen, *Nimm sein Bild in dein Herz: Geistliche Deutung eines Gemäldes von Rembrandt* (Freiburg i. Br.,

1998), 116ff. In English see Nouwen's *The Return of the Prodigal Son* (New York : Doubleday, 1992).

13. Walter Nigg, *Was bleiben soll* (Olten and Freiburg i. Br., 1973), 186.

14. Walter Nigg, *Große Heilige* (Zurich, 1947), 517.

15. C. G. Jung, *Das Geheimnis der goldenen Blüte* (Munich, 1919), 21; quoted in Anthony Storr, *C. G. Jung* (Munich, 1974), 108.

16. *Klassiker der Meditation* (Zurich, Einsiedeln, and Cologne, 1976), 48–49. In English see *Parochial and Plain Sermons*, vol. 3, sermon 9 (London, 1907).

17. Anton P. Chekhov, *Drei Schwestern* (Stuttgart, 1985), 19.

18. Eugen Drewermann, *Christ in der Gegenwart* 27 (1987): 217.

19. Fyodor M. Dostoyevsky, *Schuld und Sühne* (Munich, 1977–80), 418.

20. Manfred Hausmann, *Kleine Begegnungen mit großen Leuten* (Neukirchen-Vluyn, 1973), 105ff.

21. Francis de Sales, quoted in Drewermann, *Christ in der Gegenwart* 1 (1983): 6.

22. Michael Ramsey, *Worte an meine Priester* (Einsiedeln, 1971), 51.

23. Augustine, *Patrologia Latina* 38, 441.

24. Goethe to J. K. Lavater, July 1780, in Josef Pieper, *Über das Schweigen Goethes: Aus Goethebriefen Notiert* (Munich, 1951).

25. P. Liagre, *Retraite avec Sainte Thérèse de l'Enfant-Jésus* (Lisieux, n.d), 37.

26. Søren Kierkegaard, *Gebete*, ed. W. Rest (Cologne, 1957), 7.

27. Görres, *Das Senfkorn von Lisieux*, 102.

28. Ibid.

29. Ibid., 138.

30. Romano Guardini, *Tugenden* (Würzburg, 1963), 93–94.

31. Jean-François Six, *Theresia von Lisieux: Ihr Leben wie es wirklich war* (Freiburg i. Br., 1978), 209.

32. Martin Buber, *Schriften zum Chassidismus* (Munich and Heidelberg, 1963), 578.

33. Fyodor M. Dostoyevsky, *Der Jüngling* (Munich, 1977–80), 589–90.

34. Fyodor Dostoyevsky, *The Brothers Karamazov*, trans. Constance Garnet (New York, 1957), 294.

35. Dietrich Bonhoeffer, quoted in *Bonhoeffer Brevier*, ed. Otto Dudzus (Munich, 1968), 287–88.

36. Augustine, *Confessions* XIII, 9.

37. Görres, *Das Senfkorn von Lisieux*, 310.

38. Ibid.

39. Ibid., 522.

40. Hans Urs von Balthasar, *Schwestern im Geist* (Einsiedeln, 1970), 144.

41. Martin Buber, "Der Gang auf dem Seil," in *Schriften zum Hassidismus* (Munich and Heidelberg, 1963), 357–58.

42. Francis de Sales, *Philothea* III, 1.

43. Johann Wolfgang von Goethe, *Einleitung zur Zeitschrift "Propyläen."*

44. Thérèse of Lisieux, *Selbstbiographische Schriften*, 279.

45. Fyodor M. Dostoyevsky, *Tagebuch eines Schriftstellers* (Munich and Heidelberg, 1977–80), 334 and 34.

46. Meister Eckhart, *Deutsche Traktate*, ed. Josef Quint (Munich, 1963), 444.

47. Gerta Ital, *Der Meister, die Mönche und ich* (Munich, 1988), 5ff.

48. Augustine, *Patrologia Latina* 38, 441.

49. Eugen Roth, *Sämtliche Werke*, vol. 1, *Heitere Verse*, Part 1 (Munich and Vienna, 1977), 229.

50. Görres, *Das Senfkorn von Lisieux*, 161.

51. Fyodor M. Dostoyevsky, *Die Dämonen* (Munich, 1977–80), 957.

52. Fyodor M. Dostoyevsky, *Erinnerungen* (Munich and Zurich, 1980), 368–71; also Zenta Maurina, *Dostoijewski* (Memmingen, 1981), 154–57.

53. Cf. von Balthasar, *Schwestern im Geist*, 78.

54. Ibid., 79.

55. Augustine, *De bono viduitatis*, 21, 26.

56. Dostoyevsky, *Die Brüder Karamasoff*, 476–77.

57. von Balthasar, *Schwestern im Geist*, 64.

Sources

Histoire d'une Ame, Manuscrits autobiographiques (Paris: Éditions du Cerf–Desclée de Brouwer, 1972). In English see *Story of a Soul: The Autobiography of Saint Thérèse of Lisieux*, translated by John Clarke, 3d ed. (Washington, D.C.: ICS Publications, 1996).

Conseils et Souvenirs, collected by Sr. Geneviève de la Sainte Face, one of the saint's novices (Paris: Éditions du Cerf–Desclée de Brouwer, 1971).

Les Derniers Entretiens, last conversations of the saint with her sisters (Paris: Éditions du Cerf–Desclée de Brouwer, 1971). In English see St. Thérèse of Lisieux, *Her Last Conversations*, translated by John Clarke (Washington, D.C.: Institute of Carmelite Studies, 1977).

Les Derniers Entretiens, Volume d'Annexes (Paris: Éditions du Cerf-Desclée de Brouwer, 1971).

Les "Lettres" de Thérèse, in *Correspondence Générale*, 2 vols. (Paris: Éditions du Cerf–Desclée de Brouwer, 1972–74). In English see Saint Thérèse of Lisieux, *General Correspondence*, translated by John Clarke (Washington, D.C.: Institute of Carmelite Studies, 1982–88).

Les Poésie de Thérèse (Paris: Éditions du Cerf–Desclée de Brouwer, 1979). In English see *The Poetry of Saint Thérèse of Lisieux*, translated by Donald Kinney (Washington, D.C.: ICS Publications, Institute of Carmelite Studies, 1996).

Premier manuscrit autobiographique, dedicated to Mother Agnès de Jésus, 1895.

Second manuscrit autobiographique, September 1896.

Troisième manuscrit autobiographique, dedicated to Mother Marie de Gonzague, June–July 1897.

"Récréations pieuses," eight plays written by Thérèse from January 21, 1894, to Febuary 8, 1897, and put on by the novices.

Procès de l'ordinaire (1910–11). Rome, Teresianum.

Procès Apostololique (1915–16). Rome: Teresianum, 1976.

The quotations from Thérèse in the present volume have been translated from the German edition, which in turn are the author's translation directly from the original French texts.

Chronology

1873   Jan. 2. 11:30 p.m., birth of Marie-Françoise-Thérèse
        Martin in Alençon, capital of the Département of
        Ortie in northwest France, pop. 16,037.

        Jan. 4. Baptism in the church of Notre Dame. Her
        godmother was her eldest sister, Marie (1860–1940).

        Mar. 15–16. Thérèse is brought to a wet nurse, Rose
        Taillé in Semallé, where she will remain until April 2,
        1874.

1877   Aug. 28. Zélie Martin (b. 1831), Thérèse's mother,
        dies of breast cancer. She is buried the next day.
        Thérèse chooses her sister Pauline (1861–1951) as a
        second mother.

        Nov. 15. Thérèse leaves Alençon with her sisters and
        moves to Lisieux, where her uncle, the pharmacist
        Isidore Guérin, manages to find a new home, named
        "Les Buissonnets." The family lives there until
        Dec. 25, 1889. Thereafter the lease is not renewed.

1878   Aug. 8. At Trouville Thérèse sees the ocean for the
        first time.

1881   Oct. 3. Enters the Benedictine abbey Notre Dame du
        Pré as a halftime pupil.

1882   Oct. 2 Pauline enters the Carmelite convent in Lisieux.

1883   *May 13.* Pentecost. Thérèse is cured of a serious
        illness by the smile of the Madonna.

1884   *May 8.* First Holy Communion in the monastery; on
        the same day Pauline (Sr. Agnès de Jésus) takes her
        vows in Carmel.

1886   *Spring.* Owing to continual headaches and scruples
        Thérèse leaves the abbey school and receives lessons
        from Madame Painau.

        Oct. 15. Marie, the eldest sister, enters the Carmelite
        convent in Lisieux.

        Dec. 25. Thérèse experiences her "conversion" on
        Christmas Eve, the beginning of the third phase of
        her life.

1887   *May 1.* Her father (1823–94) suffers a first stroke,
        leading to paralysis of the legs.

        May 29. Thérèse asks her father for permission to
        enter the Carmelite convent in Lisieux; he agrees.

        July. On a Sunday in July, while gazing at a picture of
        the crucified Christ, Thérèse discovers her vocation
        to the apostolate through prayer and suffering.

        Sept. 1. Thérèse reads in the newspaper *La Croix* an
        account of the execution of the murderer Pranzini,
        for whom she had been praying since the middle of
        July, and who repented his crime in the last moments
        of his life.

        ———

Oct. 31. Trip with her father to Bayeux, to ask Bishop Hugonin for permission to enter Carmel at the age of fifteen.

Nov. 4–Dec. 12. Thérèse goes on a pilgrimage to Rome with her father and her sister Céline (1869–1959).

Nov. 20. Audience with Pope Leo XIII. Thérèse asks the pope to approve her entrance into Carmel.

Dec. 28. The bishop gives the prioress of Carmel, Mother Marie de Gonzague (1834–1904), authority to admit Thérèse.

1888   *Apr. 1.* Entrance into the Lisieux Carmel.

1889   *Jan. 10.* Takes the habit.

Feb. 12. The health of her father has deteriorated to the point that he has to be taken to the hospital of Saint-Saveur in Caen, where he will remain for two years.

Dec. 25. Les Buissonnets is given up.

1890   *Sept. 8.* Solemn vows.

1894   *July 29.* Her father dies in the castle of La Musse, which the Guérin family had inherited.

Sept. 14. Céline (Sr. Geneviève de Sainte-Thérèse) enters Carmel, the fourth of the Martin sisters to do so.

1895   *January.* Thérèse begins her "autobiographical writings."

1896   *Apr. 2–3.* The fatal disease (tuberculosis) makes its appearance with the first hemorrhage

        Apr. 5. Beginning of the test of faith.

        Sept. 8. Thérèse composes Manuscript B.

1897   *Apr. 6.* Mother Agnès de Jésus begins taking down Thérèse's last words.

        June 3. Thérèse begins, on orders from the prioress, Mother Amrie de Gonzague, to work on Manuscript C, which she breaks off some time before July 11, 1897.

        July 8. Thérèse enters the infirmary.

        July 30. Receives final anointing.

        Sept. 9. After two days of agony Thérèse dies at around 7:30 p.m. Her last words are: "My God, I love you."

1898   *Sept. 30.* First edition of the *Story of a Soul.*

1919   *October.* Cardinal Vico, prefect of the Congregation of Rites, declares: "We'd better hurry up with the glorification of the little saint if we don't want to be overtaken by the voice of the people."

1923   *Apr. 29.* Beatification by Pope Pius XI.

1925   *May 16.* Canonization by Pope Pius XI.

1927   *Dec. 14.* Pope Pius XI appoints Thérèse patroness of the missions.

1944   *May 5.* Pope Pius XII names Thérèse, along with John of Arc, patroness of France.

1997   *Oct. 19.* Elevation to Doctor of the Church by Pope John Paul II.

THE AUTHOR:

Rudolf Stertenbrink, O.P., is a friar of the Dominican order known for his powerful homilies. He has published a series of books on preaching and a selection of the writings of Thérèse of Lisieux. He resides in Hamburg, Germany.

THE BOOK:

"Little Therese" is known for an everyday simplicity that has made her the most beloved and imitated modern saint. This book reveals that she is also a true bearer of modern spirituality rooted in the stream of great thinkers from Augustine and Thomas to Dostoyevsky, Kierkegaard, and Edith Stein. Contains thoughtful, inspiring reflections. Also available from The Crossroad Publishing Company is *The Passion of Thérèse of Lisieux* by Guy Gaucher with an introduction by Benedict J. Groeschel, C.F.R. (ISBN 0-8245-0987-0).

OTHER TITLES OF INTEREST
from The Crossroad Publishing Company

Robert Barron
HEAVEN IN STONE AND GLASS
Experiencing the Spirituality of the Great Cathedrals

NOW AVAILABLE IN PAPERBACK!

"Open this book and find yourself not only placed before great art, but also thrust into an encounter with the spirituality that created the art. Robert Barron has brought the sacred, mystical space of the Gothic cathedrals to our fingertips, and in doing so has also fed our hunger for God."   — *Spiritual Book News*

0-8245-1993-0, $16.95 paperback

Henri Nouwen
LIFE OF THE BELOVED
Spiritual Living in a Secular World

NOW AVAILABLE IN PAPERBACK!

"One day while we were walking on Columbus Avenue in New York City, Fred turned to me and said, 'Why don't you write something about the spiritual life for me and my friends?' Fred's question became more than the intriguing suggestion of a young New York intellectual. It became the plea that arose on all sides — wherever I was open to hear it. And, in the end, it became for me the most pertinent and the most urgent of all demands: 'Speak to us about God.'"   — *From the Prologue*

0-8245-1184-0, $15.95 hardcover
0-8245-1986-8, $14.95 paperback

crossroad

OTHER TITLES OF INTEREST
from The Crossroad Publishing Company

Lorenzo Albacete
GOD AT THE RITZ
Attraction to Infinity

A Priest-Physicist Talks About Science, Sex,
Politics, and Religion

"*God at the Ritz* deals with the most awesome experiences of life. These experiences propel the human search for truth, beauty, justice solidarity, and personal development. They confront us with the great Mystery that always lies beyond."   — *From the Introduction*

A prominent priest and columnist for the *New York Times Sunday Magazine* offers his commentary on a variety of topics where current events and pop culture touch the spiritual: the recent bombings at the World Trade Center, the Chicken Soup series, Germaine Greer, and Charles Darwin, among others.

0-8245-1951-5, $19.95 hardcover

Guy Gaucher
THE PASSION OF THERESE OF LISIEUX

"Bishop Gaucher's haunting account of Therese's final eighteen months . . . reveals her at the summit of her journey, when she became a unique masterpiece of God's amazing grace, and the saint for the next millennium."   — Bishop Patrick V. Ahern, D.D.

Few saints enjoy the popular devotion of Therese of Lisieux. It is well-known that this twenty-four-year-old Carmelite died of tuberculosis while unpetalling roses, but what was her life really like during the critical last months? This volume is the definitive history compiled from Therese's letters and manuscripts written during this period.

0-8245-0987-0, $16.95, paperback

crossroad

OTHER TITLES OF INTEREST
from The Crossroad Publishing Company

Thomas Keating
INTIMACY WITH GOD
An Introduction to Centering Prayer

"For all those aspiring to a genuine spiritual life, Father Keating has charted a course that will take us progressively closer to our divine goal as we learn to touch God, first with the words of our lips, then with reflections of the mind and with the feelings of the heart."   — *Living Prayer*

"This is perhaps Keating's most readable and enlightening work. Filled with insight and practical advice, it offers sound wisdom on the way that centering prayer can deepen our intimacy with God."
                                        — *Spiritual Book News*

Centering prayer — you've heard about it; now learn how to do it. Keating, a Trappist monk and former abbot, teaches us this method of non-vocal prayer based on the desert fathers and mothers and the work of St. John of the Cross.

0-8245-1588-9, $16.95 paperback

Please support your local bookstore,
or call 1-800-707-0670 for Customer Service.

For a free catalog, write us at

THE CROSSROAD PUBLISHING COMPANY
481 Eighth Avenue, Suite 1550
New York, NY 10001

Visit our website at
www.crossroadpublishing.com

crossroad

Wisdom
of the
Little Flower